I0460148

The Quick and Dirty Guide to Greek Wine

Andrea Lemieux

Copyright 2025 by Andrea Lemieux
thequirkycork.com

ISBN: 979-8-9928961-0-7

Written & Designed by Andrea Lemieux
Photographs by Andrea Lemieux

All rights reserved. No part of this publication may be
reproduced, distributed, or transmitted in any form or
by any means, including photocopying, recording, or
other electronic or mechanical methods, without the
prior written permission of the author, expect in cases of
brief quotations embodied in reviews and certain other
non-commercial uses permitted by copyright law.

thequirkycork.com
@quirkycork
@thequirkycork
@thequirkycork

Acknowledgements

Huge thanks to my friends Eva Constantaras and Mauricio Reyes Cardozo who, for years, have supported my thirst for Greek wine. You've hosted me in Athens, driven me around the Peloponnese and Attica, introduced me to Oenorama, let me store wine in your apartment, and have generally been amazing and generous friends.

Big thanks to my friends Emma Aslıhan Başer Rose, Başak Gökkılıç, Malia Emiko Yoshioka, and Amber Rouse for your support and feedback!

Thank you to Anna Maria Kambourakis of Unravelling Wine and Chania Wine Tours for teaching me about Cretan wine and for making me even dream that I could do a book of any kind about Greek wine.

Thanks to Yannis Valambous, Maria Papida, and Yiannis Papaeconomou of Vassaltis Vineyards for helping expand my understanding of Santorini and its grapes.

About Me

My very first trip ever to Greece (in 2013), was before I became invested in wine. Before I knew anything other than I didn't like Chardonnay (I do now) and I didn't like Merlot (still don't). Most of what I drank on that trip was white table wine. The first Greek grape I remember drinking was Assyrtiko and, being the acid head I am, I immediately fell in love. But it

would not be until 2017, when two of my best friends moved to Athens and lured me to visit pictures of their local wine shop, that my real relationship with Greek wine began.

I never imagined writing a book about Greek wine, but here we are! While my initial book project was far more ambitious (and still in the works for the future!), the inspiration for this one struck me one night as I was

going to bed - and happily I remembered it the next morning. What kind of information do I, as a wine lover and someone deeply interested in a country's native grapes, want when I visit wine bars? I want to know about the native grapes, who works with them, what are the regions where they grow like, what can I expect from the wine, and what should I be looking for when I buy it? That is what I tried to capture here. I hope you find it as useful as I!

Table of Contents

Introduction   6

Part 1 - Native Grapes   8
Wine Styles   9
White Grapes   10
Pink/Grey Grapes   70
Black Grapes   80

Part 2 - Greek Wine Regions   120
Aegean Islands   121
Central Greece   127
Crete   132
Epirus   137
Ionian Islands   139
Macedonia   144
Peloponnese   151
Thessaly   156
Thrace   160

Part 3 - Where to Drink & Shop in Athens   163
Drink   165
Shop   168

Greek Wine Vocabulary   170

Further Reading   171

Introduction

Wine guides that cover regions in depth and/or include information about all the wineries are fantastic. But they're usually big, heavy, and just not practical to haul around with you. And, for those travelers who are planning to remain in a large city and not actively explore wine regions, not really that useful.

When beginning this project, I asked myself: what information do I want to know when I'm going to an unfamiliar wine country? For me, that is: native grapes, broad details about the wine regions, some basic vocabulary, and where to drink and buy wine.

How to use this book

The Quick and Dirty Guide to Greek Wine will help you navigate wine lists and wine shops while in Greece.

Part 1 - Native Grapes offers infographics and descriptions of some of Greece's many grapes. Quite often, even the tiniest restaurant will offer an English language food menu, but wine lists are still largely only in Greek! So you'll notice that all infographics provide both the English transliteration and Greek name for the grapes. Each description also includes recommended producers making the best example of that grape.

Part 2 - Greek Wine Regions offers a broad overview of the region's climate, geography, sub-regions, grapes, Protected Designations of Origin (PDO) and Protected Geographical Indications (PGI), and recommended producers.

Part 3 - Where to Drink & Shop in Athens, you'll find recommendations of wine bars and restaurants as well as great shops for purchasing wines.

Like the Greek grape names, the Greek vocabulary list provides a little extra help reading wine lists and labels while the Further Reading section offers a list of website and more in-depth books about Greek wine.

Γειά μας! Cheers!

Part 1

Greece's Native Grapes

Greek wine has been going through a renaissance since the 1980s with a more concentrated turn toward quality wine and native grape production. Greece claims anywhere from 200 to 350 native grapes (depending on the source you're looking at). Some grapes are so venerable, that their names have been enshrined in ancient works of literature, such as mentions of Mavroudi and Limnio in the Homeric epics.

This section, divided by white, pink, and black grapes, does NOT provide information about all of Greece's grapes! But you will find descriptions of those you are most likely to encounter.

Wines by Style

A grape's flavor profile can tell you a lot about what the wine tastes like, but maybe you're less interested in specific flavors than you are in a broad profile. Do you like aromatic wines? Maybe full-bodied and structured? Or racy acidity? The below is a quick guide to grapes that belong to a specific style.

Aromatic
- White: Kidonitsa, Moschofilero
- Black: Moschomavro

Racy/high acidity
- White: Assyrtiko (esp Santorini)
- Black: Mandilaria, Vlahiko, Xinomavro

Earthy/savory
- White: Assyrtiko,
- Black: Limnio, Limniona, Mavrodaphne, Mavro Kalavrytino, Vertzami, Xinomavro

Fruity
- White: Kidonitsa, Malagousia, Roditis, Savatiano, Vidiano,
- Black: Agiorgitiko, Kotsifali

Tannic/Structured
- White: Assyrtiko
- Black: Mavrotragano, Xinomavro

Creamy
- White: Aidani, Vidano, Robola, Vilana, Vostilidi

Powerful/Full-bodied
- Black: Avgoustiatis, Xinomavro, Mavrotragano, Vertzami, Vostilidi

Light-bodied
- White: Debina, Dafni, Kidonitsa, Lagorthi, Moschofilero, Flyto

Mineral
- White: Aidani, Assyrtiko, Lagorthi
- Black: Limniona, Vlahiko

The White Grapes

The White Grapes

Aidani	12
Asproudi	14
Assyrtiko	16
Athiri	20
Dafni	22
Debina	24
Gaidouria	26
Kakotrigis	28
Katsano	30
Kidonitsa	32
Lagorthi	36
Malagousia	38
Monemvasia	42
Plyto	44
Priknadi	46
Robola	48
Savatiano	52
Skiadopoulou	54
Skalva	56
Tachtas	58
Thrapsathiri	60
Tsaoussi	62
Vidiano	64
Vilana	66
Vostolidi	68

Aidani / Αϊδάνι

Pronunciation: eye-ee-**dthan**-ee

DESCRIPTION

Drought-resistant but susceptible to mildew. Usually blended with Assyrtiko, Aidani is making a name for its own as a varietal wine on Santorini.

ORIGIN

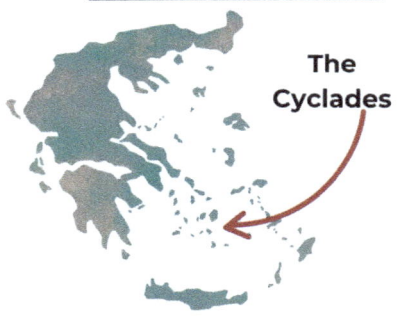

The Cyclades

PROFILE

FRUIT	BODY	TANNIN	ACIDITY
high	medium to full	medium	medium

AROMAS

citrus

peach

melon

tropical fruits

cucumber

jasmine

mineral

Aidani / Αϊδάνι

Aidani (eye-ee-**dthan**-ee) hails from The Cycladic islands of Santorini, paros, and Naxos, but is primarily grown on Santorini. Until recently, the majority of Aidani's small plantings were blended with Assyrtiko and Athiri for PDO Santorini white wines. However, there is an increasing movement on Santorini to showcase this grape on its own.

Drought-resistant, Aidani does very well on the hot and dry Cycladic islands but it is susceptible to both powdery and mildew diseases. Vines are relatively robust and produce bunches with densely-packed berries.

Generally a pale lemon-lime color, Aidani wines offer a restrained bouquet of yellow and citrus fruits, flowers, and Santorini's signature minerality. On the palate, the fruity-floral wines can offer up everything from headily perfumed flowers and citrus fruit to stone and tropical fruits. They offer a nice counterpoint to Assyrtiko's high alcohol and enamel stripping acidity with their medium-body and moderate alcohol and acidity. Santorini wineries have also begun experimenting with oak-aged and skin contact Aidani.

Aidani wines should be consumed on the younger side but high quality bottlings can age for a good five years.

- **How it's made:** dry white varietal (rare), dry white blends, vinsanto-style sweet wines
- **Where it's made:** P.D.O. Santorini, PDO Santorini Vinsanto, P.G.I. Cyclades
- **Who makes it best:** Ktima Argyros, Gavalas, Hatzidakis, Karamolegos, Vassaltis, Sigalas
- **What to eat with it:** fried zucchini; grilled white fish with lemon; Vietnamese noodle salad with cilantro and chili; eggplant salad with parsley, green salads, saganaki

Asproudi / Ασπρούδι

Pronunciation: ah-**sproo**-dthee

DESCRIPTION

Also known as 'Asproudes', this is actually a blend of white grapes, not a single varietal that creates simple but refreshing wines.

ORIGIN

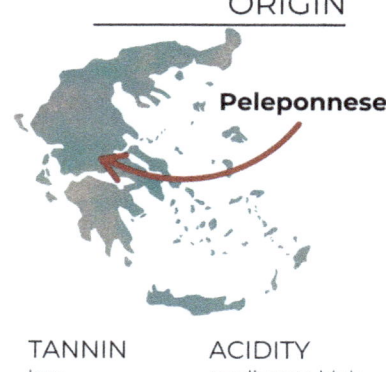

Peleponnese

PROFILE

FRUIT
medium

BODY
medium

TANNIN
low

ACIDITY
medium to high

AROMAS

citrus

pear

floral

Asproudi / Ασπρούδι

Asproudi (ah-**sproo**-dthee), or Asproudes, is a difficult grape to discuss, precisely because it is not a grape. It is, in fact, a group of grapes. The name itself merely means "whites" in Greek. These are grapes that are planted, harvested, and fermented together.

Once considered to be a single grape variety, it was Professor B D Krimbas in his Greek Ampelography, written in the 1940s, who described 12 Asproudi, most of which distinguished by a place name, such as 'Asproudes of Serres'. Cultivated mostly in the Peloponnese, Asproudes also pops up in the central and western parts of Greece as well as some of the Ionian and Aegean islands.

Our current understanding of Asproudi is thanks largely to Yorgos Tsimbidis of Monemvasia Winery who worked with a group of researchers from the Hellenic Agricultural Organisation DIMITRA and the Agricultural University of Athens.

Asproudi wines are light and fresh and best consumed within the first couple years after harvest.

- **How it's made:** dry white wine
- **Where it's made:** P.D.O. Mantinia, P.G.I. Laconia, P.G.I Serres
- **Who makes it best:** Monemvasia Winery, Ktima Brintziki, Domaine Nerantzi, Antonopoulos Vineyards, Markogiannis Winery
- **What to eat with it:** as an aperitif, creamy pastas, lemon dressings, green salads, light fish/seafood

Assyrtiko / Ασύρτικο

Pronunciation: ah-**seer**-tee-koh

DESCRIPTION

Flagship white grape of
Greece. Originates in the
volcanic soils of Santorini
but has spread across the
country. Late-ripening,
heat resistant, prone to
oxidation.

ORIGIN

Santorini

PROFILE

FRUIT	BODY	TANNIN	ACIDITY
medium	medium to full	low to medium	high

AROMAS

lemon/citrus

lime

stone fruit

green apple

lemongrass

white pepper

beeswax

honey

sea spray

mineral

brown spices

Assyrtiko / Ασύρτικο

Practically synonymous with Santorini, Assyrtiko (ah - **seer** - tee- koh) is possibly one of the greatest white grape varieties in the Mediterranean. Its immense popularity has not orly resulted in the grape's spread across Greece (and even outside!) but also greatly contributed to the rise and popularity of Greek wine overall.

Assyrtiko is resistant to most diseases and to drought, especially important on Santorini. The vine's hardwood contributes to its flexibility helping it to withstand strong winds. Famously, most vineyards on Santorini, especially the old ones, house vines trained in baskets, or *kouloura* and *kladeftiko*. This style of training provides further protection from the island's intense winds while also collecting morning dew, scme years the only precipitation the vines get.

Santorini vines are old, very old. While the trunks we see above ground may be as old as 100 years, it is difficult to tell how old the root systems are. When the vine becomes too old to produce quality fruit, it is possible to cut it off at its base and graft a new vine onto the existing root system. Working in this way, it is not impossible for Santorini Assyrtiko root systems to be 300 years old, or older.

Wines from Assyrtiko, especially those from Santorini, show high alcohol balanced by often searing acidity. It is more of a textural variety, emphasizing extract, body and structure, rather than an aromatic grape. Often austere in its youth, classic, unoaked Assyrtiko offers flavors of citrus, green apple, stone fruit, sea spray, and minerality while wines from outside Santorini keep the crispness but it shows a greater level of primary fruit aromas and a less dense structure.

It is a versatile grape that takes well to many different winemaking techniques. The classic unoaked and taut style can be tamed by extended lees ageing, while oak ageing rounds out the acidity and adds a creamy complexity. Some producers have also started experimenting with wine aged in vessels such as cement eggs and clay amphora. Skin contact/amber Assyrtiko wines are also on the rise with several remarkable examples coming out of mainland Greece.

Producers both on Santorini and elsewhere in Greece are making excellent sparkling wine with the grape, and Santorini's famous and historic sweet Vinsanto must also be mentioned.

Assyrtiko not only can age well, five to ten years to start, but especially those coming from Santorini should be aged for one to two years before drinking.

- **How it's made:** dry varietal wines, blends, skin-contact, sparkling, sweet wines, Vinsanto
- **Where it's made*:** P.D.O. Santorini, P.D.O. Slopes of Meliton, P.D.O. Handakas - Candia, P.D.O. Rhodes, P.D.O. Monemvasia - Malvasia, P.D.O. Malvasia Paros, P.D.O. Malvasia Sitia, P.D.O. Malvasia Handakas - Candia, P.G.I. Macedonia, P.G.I. Avdira, P.G.I. Attiki, P.G.I. Crete, P.G.I. Drama, P.G.I. Cyclades, P.G.I. Pieria, P.G.I. Korinthia, P.G.I. Gerania, P.G.I. Heraklion, P.G.I. Meteora, P.G.I. Thiva, P.G.I. Serres
- **Who makes it best:**
  - From Santorini: Estate Argyros, Art Space, Canava Chrissou & Tselepos, Gai'a, Gavalas Winery, Estate Hatzidakis, Karamolegos, Mikra Thira, Santo Wines, Domaine Sigalas, Vassaltis Vineyards, Venetsanos
  - Other islands: T-Oinos, Lyrarakis, Patoinos, Moraitis, Syrou Winery, Vriniotis

- Mainland Greece: Alpha Estate, Biblia Chora, Wine Art, Kechris and Gikas (Retsina), Markogianni Winery, Moschopolis Winery, Navitas Winery, Papargyriou
- **What to eat with it :** The vast range of style both mean that Assyrtiko can pair with a vast range of food, but also that you need to take the style into consideration for the pairing. Seafood is of course a classic pairing but its high acidity also makes it great for cutting through richer dishes.

Not exhaustive, Assyrtiko is grown everywhere and many PDOs and PGIs account for its use in varietal and blended wines.

Athiri / Αθήρι

Pronunciation: ah-**thee**-ree

DESCRIPTION

Athiri is one of the oldest varieties planted in the Aegean Islands. Difficult to find as a varietal wine, Athiri is usually blended with Assyrtiko and Aidani.

ORIGIN

Aegean Islands

PROFILE

FRUIT	BODY	TANNIN	ACIDITY
medium	medium	low	low

AROMAS

citrus blossom

citrus

lemon

green fruits

stone fruit

Athiri / Αθήρι

One theory posits that Athiri (ah-**thee**-ree) both hails from and takes its name from Santorini which is also known as Thira. Whether or not that is true, it is one of the oldest grapes from the Aegean Islands, planted largely in the Dodecanese and Cyclades and now found here and there across Greece.

Athiri is a thin-skinned and vigorous variety. It ripens early and timing harvest is of particular importance for this grape as it loses acidity very quickly. Already a grape with merely soft acidity, if left too long on the vine, resulting wines will be flabby.

Rarely will you find a varietal wine made with this grape. Partially because plantings are so low, but also because its lower acidity level makes it more difficult to craft into quality wine. The majority of Athiri planted on Santorini therefore is destined to become part of a PDO Santorini blend with the more powerful Assyrtiko and Aidani.

Finding a varietal Athiri is not an easy task as its simplicity and lower acidity levels leave it largely destined to be folded into white blends.

Lightly aromatic with aromas of yellow fruits, lemon, grapefruit, and citrus blossom, Athiri gives medium-bodied wines with moderate alcohol and soft acidity best drunk young within a few years of bottling.

- **How it's made:** white blends, varietal white wines
- **Where it's from:** P.D.O. Slopes of Meliton, P.D.O. Rhodes, P.D.O. Santorini, P.D.O. Handakas Candia, P.D.O. Malvasia Sitia, P.D.O. Malvasia Handakas Candia
- **Who makes it best:** Ktima Argyros, Santo Wines
- **What to eat with it:** as an aperitif, green salads, light/delicate dishes

Dafni / Δαφνί

Pronunciation: dtha-**fnee**

DESCRIPTION

Named for the laurel (bay) plant that gives the wine its distinctive herbaceous aroma, Dafni produces powerful wines with moderate alcohol.

ORIGIN

Crete

PROFILE

FRUIT	BODY	TANNIN	ACIDITY
medium	medium	low	medium

AROMAS

citrus

tropical fruits

stone fruit

ginger

floral

laurel

rosemary

thyme

sage

Dafni / Δαφνί

Crete has recently been behind the resurrection of several grape varieties. One such grape, thanks to Lyrarakis Wines, is the white Dafni (dtha-**fnee**).

Dafni is a vigorous and high-yielding variety making attention to vines during the growing season with activities such as green-harvesting and pruning, vital for winemakers looking to make quality wine. Working in their favor though, is the grape's hardy character. Thick skins give it resistance to drought and fungal diseases. The conical bunches of large, yellow-green berries are loosely structured allowing for airflow which additionally helps with disease resistance. Dafne does not reach full ripeness until late in the season and is often harvested as late as October.

Native around Crete's Heraklion, the grape takes its name from the Greek word for 'laurel', a nod to its distinctly herbal aroma profile. In addition to aromatic herbs, you'll find a complement of flowers, stone fruit, and yellow and white fruit.

Dafni wines are dry and light to medium-bodied with low/moderate alcohol and acidity, and great structure. Due to its recent more high-profile status, winemakers rarely blend Dafni, but some are experimenting with barrel fermentation and ageing. Most wines should be consumed young, within three years of bottling, but there are a few higher quality examples out there with enough complexity that they can age an additional few years.

- **How it's made:** dry white varietal
- **Where it's made:** P.G.I. Crete
- **Who makes it best:** Douloufakis Winery, Kir Yianni, Lyrarakis Wines
- **What to eat with it:** It is a great match to intense yet light summer dishes, like pastas and salads as well as salt and pepper calamari and spanakopita.

Debina / Ντεμπίνα

Pronunciation: de-**bee**-nah

DESCRIPTION

Debina creates fresh
and dry wines with a
predominate Granny
Smith apple character
but also is increasingly
used for sparkling
wines.

ORIGIN

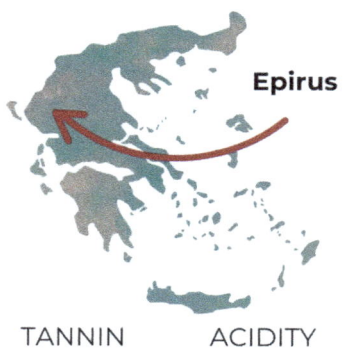

Epirus

PROFILE

FRUIT	BODY	TANNIN	ACIDITY
medium to high	light to medium	low	medium to high

AROMAS

lemon

citrus

peach

green apple

pear

Debina / Ντεμπίνα

Debina (de-**bee**-nah) is not a grape you'll see everywhere. Hailing from the mountainous area Zitsa in Epirus, this grape is increasing in popularity but has yet to hit the main stage.

An especially sensitive grape, Debina grows well in the cold, northwestern mountain climate of Epirus where it can easily achieve its naturally high levels of acidity during the growing season. It can lose acidity rapidly through and needs to be carefully monitored to properly time harvest, usually at the end of September or early October.

It gives fresh and light-bodied wines with low alcohol. Debina wines are most associated with crisp, green apple flavors but can also show pear, stone fruit, and bright citrus. Debina wines are not commonly blended and created mostly as dry whites as well sparkling and semi-sparkling wines, however a few producers are experimenting with skin contact/amber styles.

- **How it's made:** dry white, semi-dry white, sparkling, semi-sparkling
- **Where it's made:** P.D.O. Zitsa
- **Who makes it best:** Glinavos, Zoinos
- **What to eat with it:** light, aperitif-style dishes, white meats, fish, spanakopita, delicate flavored cheeses

Gaidouria / Γαϊδουριά

Pronunciation: guy-dthoo-ree-**ya**

DESCRIPTION

A rare grape from The Cyclades, today it mostly makes up minute portions of white wine blends from Santorini.

ORIGIN

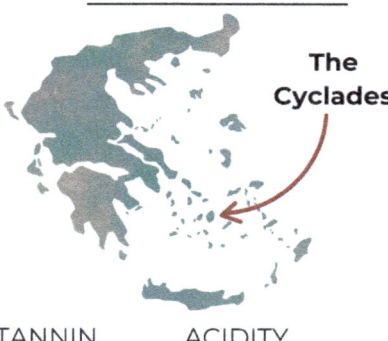

The Cyclades

PROFILE

FRUIT	BODY	TANNIN	ACIDITY
medium	medium	medium	medium

AROMAS

lemon

stone fruit

white flowers

honey

Gaidouria / Γαϊδούρια

Gaidouria (guy-**dthoo**-ree-ya) is one of the oldest grapes in the Cyclades, but also one of the rarest.

Also commonly spelled Gaidoura, it masquerades under a few other names including Gaidouricha, Gaidouriha, and Guydourina. There are also limited plantings in Turkey where it goes by the name Gaydura.

Gaidouria takes its name from the Greek word for donkey, gaidoura, supposedly because the animals are especially fond of the grape's leaves.

Vines are vigorous and relatively disease-resistant, but only mildly productive. Grapes ripen early but can attain high sugar levels while retaining moderate acidity.

What little Gaidouria is produced can usually be found blended with Katsano and creates aromatic and lightly tannic wines.

Native to the Cyclades, it is cultivated in small quantities on Santorini where, together with Katsano, covers less than 1% of all vineyard area.

- **How it's made:** dry, white wine blends
- **Where it's made:** P.G.I. Cyclades
- **Who makes it best**: Ktima Flamourou, Ktima Gavalas
- **What to eat with it:** green salads, haloumi, light seafood and white fish, steamed pork dumplings

Kakotrigis / Κακοτρύγης

Pronunciation: kah-koe-**tree**-geese

DESCRIPTION

Concentrated mainly on
Corfu, Kakotrigis creates
medium-bodied, lemon-
scented wines with
moderate and
refreshing acidity.

ORIGIN

Ionian Islands

PROFILE

FRUIT	BODY	TANNIN	ACIDITY
medium to high	medium to high	low	medium

AROMAS

lemon

melon

lemon blossom

honeycomb

lemongrass

Kakotrigis / Κακοτρύγης

Kakotrigis (kah-koe-**tree**-geese) is a portmanteau of two words: kako meaning bad and trigis harvest. The grape earned its name, not because it gives bad harvests, but because it is difficult to harvest having very hard stems that require extra effort to cut.

Late-budding but early-ripening, Kakotrigis is native to the Ionian Islands, specifically Corfu. Its vines produce small berries and large, compact bunches. High-yielding and vigorous, it is susceptible to downy mildew and insect bites. Despite the short maturing period, the grapes accumulate high amounts of sugar leading to wines rich in alcohol with moderate acidity.

- **How it's made:** dry white and skin contact/amber wines
- **Where it's made:** P.G.I. Corfu
- **Who makes it best:** Diamantopoulos Winery, Goulis Winery, Gramenos Family Winery, Pontiglio Winery
- **What to eat with it:** green salads, seafood, white fish, light foods

Katsano / Κατσανό

Pronunciation: kaht-sah-**no**

DESCRIPTION

A rare variety, on Santorini, Katsano produces medium-bodied wines with good acidity and a fruity-floral profile.

ORIGIN

The Cyclades

PROFILE

FRUIT	BODY	TANNIN	ACIDITY
medium to high	medium to high	low	medium

AROMAS

lemon

stone fruit

tropical fruit

pineapple

lemon blossom

honey

salt

Katsano / Κατσανό

Katsano (kaht-sah-**no**) is a very rare white grape variety from the Cyclades. An old grape, it is one of the 50 or so varieties once grown on Santorini. Today, however, Katsano, together with Gaidouria, cover less than 1% of Santorini's vineyards.

Usually blended with Gaidouria, Katsano produces wines with good acidity, sweet lemony, stone fruit, and floral aromas.

- **How it's made:** dry, white wine blends
- **Where it's made:** P.G.I. Cyclades
- **Who makes it best:** Ktima Gavalas
- **What to eat with it:** green salads, haloumi, light seafood and white fish, steamed pork dumplings

Kidonitsa / Κυδωνίτσα

Pronunciation: kee-dthoe-**neet**-sah

DESCRIPTION

Also spelled 'Kydonitsa', takes its name from its most distinctive aroma "kidoni' or quince. Its medium-bodied wines have crisp acidity and are intensely aromatic.

ORIGIN

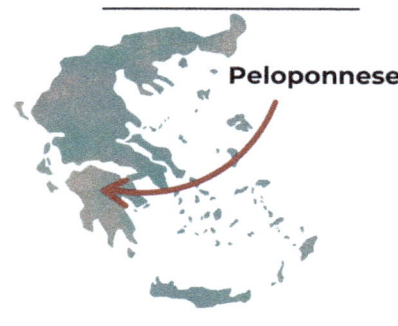

Peloponnese

PROFILE

FRUIT	BODY	TANNIN	ACIDITY
high	medium	low	medium to high

AROMAS

bergamot

orange

pear

quince

tropical fruit

floral

chamomile

mineral

Kidonitsa / Κυδωνίτσα

Kidonitsa (kee-dthoe-**neet**-sah), also spelled Kydonitsa, is one of the most well-known of the re-emergent Greek varieties from the last 15 years. Originating in Laconia in the south-east of the Peloponnese, Kidonitsa's reemergence is thanks largely to Giorgos Tsimpidis of Monemvasia Winery and Giorgos Theodorakakos of Theodorakakos. Unlike a lot of currently re-emerging varieties, Kidonitsa was not hovering on the edge of extinction, merely buried in mixed vineyards. Due to growing in mixed vineyards, obtaining pure Kidonitsa wines was difficult and expensive. That is until producers like Tsimpidis and Theodorakakos began to make substantial new plantings of the grape on its own.

A lightly pink-tinged grape, Kidonitsa can be high-yielding so wineries need to control growth to ensure quality wine. In Nemea, for example, it is not uncommon for producers to conduct two rounds of green harvest. Kidonitsa s drought resistant and grows well in dry farmed vineyards. Additionally, it has high disease resistance, except in the cases of oicium.

While nothing can compare to the popularity of Agiorgitiko in the Peloponnese, Kidonitsa enjoys its own share of acclaim.

The grape takes its name from the Greek word *kidoni* meaning quince, the wine's dominant note. The lemon colored wines are intensely aromatic with notes of quince, pear, bergamot, orange, flowers, and some minerality. Wines are medium-bodied with moderate alcohol and crisp acidity. While a few producers are experimenting with barrel ageing, the grape oxidizes easily, so is most often fermented and matured in closed stainless steel tanks. Some producers also age the wine on its lees for a period of months to add more weight and roundness.

Generally Kidonitsa should be drunk young but the best examples can age up to three to five years. pasta, spicy foods, salty white cheeses, stuffed grape leaves.

- **How it's made:** dry varietal white wines, dry white blends, sweet blends
- **Where it's made:** P.D.O. Monemvasia-Malvasia, P.G.I. Lakonia, P.G.I. Macedonia, P.G.I. Peleponnese
- **Who makes it best:** Monemvasia, Theodorakakos, Ieropoulos, Papagiannakopoulos, Aslanis, Bairaktaris, Ligas, Zaharias, Gofas, Nikolaou, Vatistas Ioannis Winery, Oenops
- **What to eat with it:** fish/seafood, white poultry, salads, white pasta, spicy foods, salty white cheeses, stuffed grape leaves

Lagorthi / Λαγόρθι

Pronunciation: la-**gore**-thee

DESCRIPTION

A lesser-known variety, Lagorthi's wines are light-bodied, crisp, with low alcohol, and distinctly mineral. Often citrussy and floral, they are capable of aging for some years.

ORIGIN

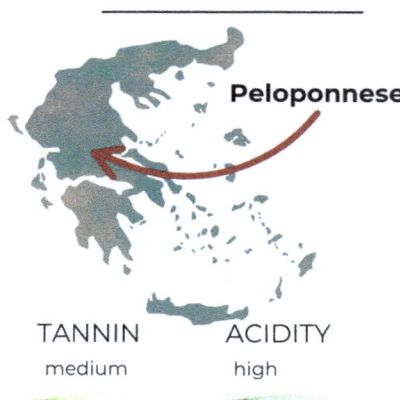

Peloponnese

PROFILE

FRUIT	BODY	TANNIN	ACIDITY
medium	medium	medium	high

AROMAS

citrus

pear

wild herbs

white flowers

sweet hay

mineral

Lagorthi / Λαγόρθι

Lagorthi is a lesser-known variety found mainly in Achaia and Kalavryta making a slow comeback. While there is a smattering of Lagorthi plantings on some of the Ionian islands, the grape is generally confined to just a few vineyards in the northern Peloponnese.

It is sensitive to water stress but otherwise generally disease resistant and relatively vigorous. A late-ripening grape reaching full ripeness around the end of September, Lagorthi manages to reach maturity and flavor at low sugar levels, at 12% or lower. The berries have thick skins and a fairly low juice content creating a perfect storm of a demanding vinification process, which is likely what led to the grape's decline in popularity. It wouldn't be until the 1980s and pioneering producer Constantinos Antonopoulos that varietal Lagorth hit the quality wine shelves.

Lagorthi is being revived to bring us an outstanding special white wine with a unique charm.

Lagorthi's wines are pale, silver-yellow with moderately intense but elegant aromas focusing on minerality and florality. The palate is lean, coming across with great purity, with high acidity and low alcohol. Almost never aged in oak, Lagorth is sometimes blended or even fermented on the skins and aged in clay amphorae.

Wines are usually consumed within three years, but the best examples can be age worthy, up to eight years or more.

- **How it's made:** dry varietal white wines, dry white blends
- **Where it's made:** P.G.I. Slopes of Aigialeia
- **Who makes it best:** Rouvalis, M20, Kanakaris Winery
- **What to eat with it:** fish/seafood, white poultry, salads, lemony sauces, spanakopita

Malagousia / Μαλαγουζιά

Pronunciation: mah-lah-goo-zee-**ya**

DESCRIPTION

Also spelled 'Malagouzia',
this highly aromatic
grape owes its
resurgence in the 1970s
to the Gerovassiliou
estate.

ORIGIN

Central Greece

PROFILE

FRUIT	BODY	TANNIN	ACIDITY
high	medium	low	medium

AROMAS

stone fruits

tropical fruits

grapefruit

lime

green pepper

aromatic herbs

floral

Malagousia / Μαλαγουζιά

Malagousia (mah-lah-goo-zee-**ya**), is one of Greece's early grape revival success stories. In the 1970's the grape (also spelled Malagouzia) was virtually unknown. At the time, professor of oenology, Dr. Logothetis gave some vine cuttings to a student of his, Evangelos Gerovassiliou. Thanks to Gerovassiliou's dedication, Malagousia is now one of Greece's most well-known and respected varieties.

Iso instrumental to the grape's success was Roxani Matsa from Matsas Estate in Attica. While Gerovassiliou did the, shall we say heavy lifting, Malagousia's spread across Greece is down to Matsa who gave away vine cuttings to any interested growers.

Malagousia is a high-yielding variety with heavy bunches crowded with big berries. Because of its thin skin and compact clusters, the grape is prone to a number of diseases and insect attacks. It does well in dry conditions and low fertility soils, both of which have the advantage of controlling the grape's vigor. Malagousia ripens early giving one of the earliest harvests in Greece in mid to late August, although plantings in cooler areas may not ripen until mid-September.

Widely believed to have originated in Central Greece, Malagousia vines have spread across the country and even to some of the islands. It has proven to be adaptable to different climates around the country, and shows a different character depending on where it grows. Macedonia's harsher, colder climate gives later harvests and more linear, herbaceous expressions. In warmer Central Greece and Attica, wines are intensely aromatic. Malagousia has even spread to several of the islands, notably Paros and Rhodes.

Malagousia makes medium pale, lemon-lime color wines that are highly aromatic. Depending on where it's grown, wines range from herbal, citrussy, and green to exotic fruits and ripe stone fruit but are always floral. On the palate, wines are medium-bodied and round with a supple texture and fresh acidity, with generally high alcohol.

The majority of Malagousia wines are vinified in stainless steel tanks, but a smaller portion is also fermented and/or aged in oak barrels. A few winemakers are also experimenting with sparkling, amphora aged, and skin contact/amber wines. Sweet Malagousia usually comes from late harvest grapes which additionally emphasize the variety's intense aromas.

- **How it's made:** dry varietal wines, dry blends, sweet wines
- **Where it's made*:** P.D.O. Rhodes, P.G.I. Cyclades, P.G.I. Pallini, P.G.I. Attiki, P.G.I. Central Greece, P.G.I. Epanomi, P.G.I. Tyrnavos, P.G.I. Slopes of Aegialia, P.G.I. Atalanti Valley, P.G.I. Meteora, P.G.I. Florina, P.G.I. Pieria, P.G.I. Lakonia
- **Who makes it best:** Alpha, Anatolikos Vineyards, Boutari (Matsa), Chrisostomou, Gerovassiliou, Karadimos, Kitrus, Lazaridi, Lykos, Moschopolis Winery, Mylonas, Papagiannakos, Papagianni, Tetramythos, Theopetra, Volacus, Wine Art, Zafeirakis
- **What to eat with it:**
  - (with dry wines) stuffed cabbage leaves with rice, risotto, salads, artichokes, fatty fish, roasted poultry, cream sauces
  - (with sweet wines) spicy curry, fruit or custard-based desserts

While extensive, this is not an exhaustive list

Monemvasia /
Μονεμβασιά

Pronunciation: mone-em-vah-see-**ya**

DESCRIPTION

Mildly aromatic
wines with medium
body and moderate
acidity and alcohol.
Monemvasia wines
can be dry or sweet.

ORIGIN

Peloponnese

PROFILE

FRUIT	BODY	TANNIN	ACIDITY
medium	medium to full	low	low to medium

AROMAS

lemon blossom

lemon

citrus

peach

green fruits

spice

Monemvasia / Μονεμβασιά

Monemvasia (mone-em-vah-see-**ya**), or Malvasia as you may also see it, has an interesting story. Not named after the port city of the same name, it originated in the Peloponnesian district of Lakonia; but today mostly grows in the Cyclades, particularly on Paros.

In the vineyard, Monemvasia is a high-yielding variety, largely resistant to disease and drought. It is a grape that you really have to want to work with though. Extremely prone to oxidation, winemakers need to protect it at every step of the harvest and winemaking process. This difficulty may partially explain why the grape went out of fashion, and nearly out of existence, in the 20th century.

Careful handling produces medium-bodied wines with moderate alcohol, low to medium acidity, and semi-aromatic notes of citrus, white fruits, stone fruit, flowers, and spice. Monemvasia stands out as the only variety allowed in the production of PDO red wines (PDO Paros) in which winemakers blend it with Mandilaria.

- **How it's made:** dry white wine, sweet wine, dry red wine, dry rosé
- **Where it's made:** P.D.O. Paros, P.D.O. Monemvasia-Malvasia, P.D.O. Malvasia Paros, P.G.I. Monemvasia
- **Who makes it best:** Monemvasia Winery, Ktima Kir Yianni
- **What to eat with it:** as an aperitif, with light salads, young cheeses

Plyto / Πλυτό

Pronunciation: plee-**toe**

DESCRIPTION

The rare Plyto makes light to medium bodied wines with mouthwatering, lemony acidity and fruity-green notes.

ORIGIN

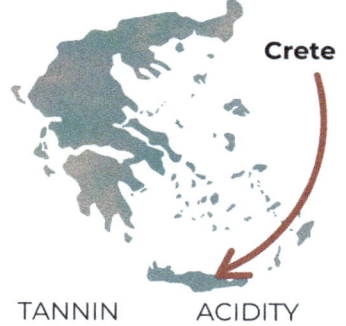

Crete

PROFILE

FRUIT	BODY	TANNIN	ACIDITY
medium	light	low	medium to high

AROMAS

lemon

grapefruit

peach

green apple

herbal

vegetal

honeysuckle

white tea

Plyto / Πλυτό

These days, if you want an unusual or resurrected grape, the best place to head is Crete. The island has brought several grapes back to life over the last few years, including Plyto (plee-**toe**). Rare even on Crete, Plyto comes from Heraklion where it was found hiding in old Vilana and Liatiko vineyards in the 1990s. Once discovered, Heraklion area wineries threw themselves behind identifying vines and replanting them and propagating new vines.

The older Plyto vines grow in bush/goblet trained shapes, with the new plantings being trained to the more modern wire and VSP system. It's a vigorous vine that prefers clay-loam soils and has good resistance to dry conditions. The large bunches however, are susceptible to downy mildew and botrytis bunch rot.

Its wines are light-bodied with moderate alcohol, mouthwatering acidity, and aromas of lemon, grapefruit, peach, and aromatic herbs. They do gain more depth with some ageing but still should be drunk within the first three to four years.

- **How it's made:** dry white varietal and blend wines
- **Where it's made:** P.G.I. Iraklion
- **Who makes it best:** Lyrarakis Wines
- **What to eat with it:** green salads, lemon orzo, light seafood, halloumi

Priknadi / Πρικνάδι

Pronunciation: prek-**nah**-dee

DESCRIPTION

Priknadi, or Preknadi, gives aromatic, fruity wines full of tropical, stone, and citrus fruit with underlying minerality.

ORIGIN

Macedonia

PROFILE

FRUIT	BODY	TANNIN	ACIDITY
high	medium	low	medium to high

AROMAS

citrus

green apple

mango

pear

stone fruit

white pepper

mineral

Priknadi / Πρικνάδι

Hailing from the Naoussa area of Macedonia in Greece's north, Priknadi (prek-**nah**-dee) has more names than it does producers. This hard to find grape may also be listed as Preknadi (most common), Prekiadi, Prekna, Preknari, Preknari Lefkp, Prekniariko, or Prekno.

Producers extensively cultivated Priknadi in Naoussa until the 1960s when phylloxera hit the region, decimating the majority of Priknadi vineyards. Only recently have producers started trying to resurrect the variety. The grape's name comes from the Greek word *prekniaris* (freckle face), a perfect description of the grape's freckled skin. In the vineyard it is resistant to drought but susceptible to botrytis.

Priknadi wines tend to be rather high in alcohol with medium acidity and an aromatic nose of stone and tropical fruit, tree fruit, citrus, and mineral. Mostly you'll find younger wines on the market now, but Priknadi can develop beautifully over a few years.

- **How it's made:** dry white wines
- **Where it's made:** P.G.I. Imathia
- **Who makes it best:** Ktima Diamantakos, Ktima Chrysohoou
- **What to eat with it:** risotto and white sauce pasta, poultry, salads and Asian cuisine

Robola / Ρομπόλα

Pronunciation: row-**bow**-lah

DESCRIPTION

Robola creates elegant and complex wines with excellent texture and steely acidity.

PROFILE

FRUIT
medium to high

BODY
medium

TANNIN
medium

ACIDITY
high

ORIGIN

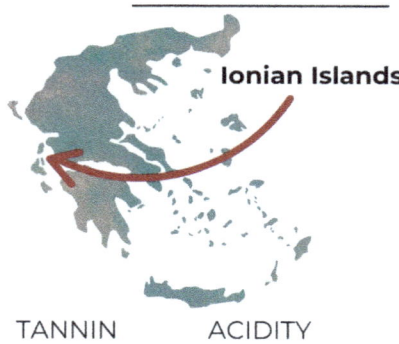

Ionian Islands

AROMAS

grapefruit

citrus

lemon

fennel

earthy

Robola / Ρομπόλα

From the Ionian Island, Cephalonia, Robola (row-**bow**-lah) was for years confused with Italian grape, Ribolla Gialla; but recent genetic tests have certified there is no relationship between the two and that Robola is 100% Greek. It does still nod to Italy in a way, having taken the moniker *'vino di sasso'* or 'wine from stones' because of where it grows.

Cephalonia is the main home of Robola, although limited plantings exist on other Ionian islands and in Macedonia and the Peloponnese. Vines on Cephalonia are often planted ungrafted in the island's poor, stony, limestone soils.

Here on the island, one can still find old, bush vine vineyards attesting to the grape's history.

Robola is an early-ripening, vigorous, and high-yielding variety with small berries that grow in small clusters. It is susceptible to drought as well as powdery mildew, botrytis, and other viruses.

Prone to oxidation, Robola must be treated with care. Most often vinified in stainless steel tanks, winemakers often age the wine on its lees or in oak to add depth and body. Wines are not overly aromatic but have interesting notes of citrus, tree fruit, fennel, herbs, and mineral. Depending on how it is made (e.g. with lees contact and/or oak or not), wines can range from steely with crisp acidity to rounder and fuller-bodied. The former style should be drunk within the first three years after harvest, but the more complex wines can age at least five to six years.

An interesting note about Robola on labels: P.D.O. Robola of Cephalonia is the only dry wine appellation in Greece that refers to a single grape variety and not just a region. Additionally, 'Robola' cannot appear on any label outside of the P.D.O.

- **How it's made:** dry white wine
- **Where it's made:** P.D.O. Robola of Cephalonia (Kefalonia)
- **Who makes it best:** Gentilini Winery, Orealios Gaea, Petrakopoulos, Sclavos, Saris, Foivos
- **What to eat with it:** white fish, seafood, white meat poultry, lemon dressing

Savatiano / Σαββατιανό

Pronunciation: sav-vah-tee-ah-**no**

DESCRIPTION

The most planted grape of Attica, Savatiano is mostly known as the retsina grape but has been making a serious comeback as a quality wine.

ORIGIN

Attica

PROFILE

FRUIT	BODY	TANNIN	ACIDITY
medium to high	medium	low	medium to high

AROMAS

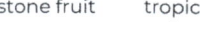  

stone fruit   tropical fruit   green fruits   citrus

floral   grass   mineral

Savatiano / Σαββατιανό

Savatiano (sav-vah-tee-ah-**no**) or, Savvatiano, is one of - if not the! - most maligned grapes in Greece. Why? Because, for years, Savatiano was used almost exclusively to make cheap Retsina. And while well-made Retsina can be a delight, the cheap stuff, and the grape behind it, is a shadow from behind which the Greek wine industry has only recently(ish) managed to emerge. Despite its poor reputation, Savatiano can craft excellent still and semi-sparkling wines. Something a handful of producers in Central Greece, have thrown themselves into doing.

One of the most popular varieties in Greece, Savatiano plantings are concentrated in eastern Central Greece, especially Attica where it takes up some 80% of total grape plantings. The grape is resistant to mildew diseases and performs well in drought conditions.

Savatiano wines offer flavors ranging from yellow fruit, apples, stone fruit, and flowers with fresh acidity. Basic wines should be drunk within one to two years of harvest, but more complex wines, for example those aged in oak or made from old, bush vines, are ageing well. High-quality, aged Savatiano takes on honeyed and nutty flavors and a deeper texture. While you're safe hanging onto such bottles for as many as eight years, some Attica wineries suggest these might age even longer. Well-made Savatiano also has the advantage of being a great food wine.

- **How it's made:** dry white wines, white blends, Retsina, semi-sparkling wine
- **Where it's made:** P.G.I. Slopes of Kithaironas, P.G.I. Attiki, P.G.I. Karystos, P.G.I. Retsina of Mesogia Traditional Appellation
- **Who makes it best:** Aoton, Frangou, Kokotos, Markou, Matsa Mylonas, Nikolou, Vassiliou, Papagiannakos, Akriotou Microwinery, Muses Estate, Samartzis
- **What to eat with it:** fatty fish and seafood, white poultry, pasta salads, potato salads, green salads, risotto, white pastas

Skiadopoulou / Σκιαδόπουλο

Pronunciation: (ski-ya-**dtho**-poo-low)

DESCRIPTION

Produced as both a varietal wine and in the Verdea blends, it gives wines with citrus, tropical, and herbal aromas high in acidity, with a pleasing oiliness.

ORIGIN

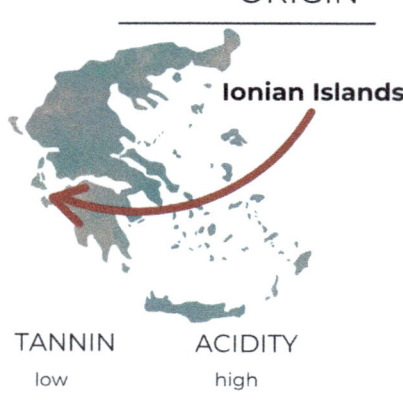

Ionian Islands

PROFILE

FRUIT	BODY	TANNIN	ACIDITY
high	medium to high	low	high

AROMAS

lemon   lime   mango   tropical fruit

lemon blossom   grass   aromatic herbs

Skiadopoulou / Σκιαδόπουλο

Skiadopoulou / Σκιαδόπουλο (ski-ya-**dtho**-poo-low) from the Ionian Islands has a number of other names, including: Skiadopoulous, Skiadopoylo, Zachara, Zacharo, Zahara, and Zakynthino. The latter of which is confusing as Zakynthino is also a completely different variety.

A white color mutation of the black Fokiano grape, Skiadopoulou is produced as a varietal white wine and lends itself to blended wines, most notably the traditional Verdea blend of Zakynthos. Bright acidity balances a subtle oiliness on the palate which lingers with citrus and tropical fruit flavors framed by flowers and soft herbs.

- **How it's made:** dry, white varietal wines and blends
- **Where it's made:** P.G.I. Slopes of Ainos, P.G.I. Zakyrthos
- **Who makes it best:** Achaia Clauss, Ktima Antonopoulos, Ktima Grampsa, Oenolpi Winery
- **What to eat with it:** grilled fish or seafood, poultry, pork in lemon sauce, lobster, green salads with lemony dressing

Sklava / Σκλάβα

Pronunciation: **sklah**-vah

DESCRIPTION

A rare grape produced entirely by Zacharias Vineyards, Sklava creates an expressive wine with a noticeably oily texture and refreshing acidity.

ORIGIN

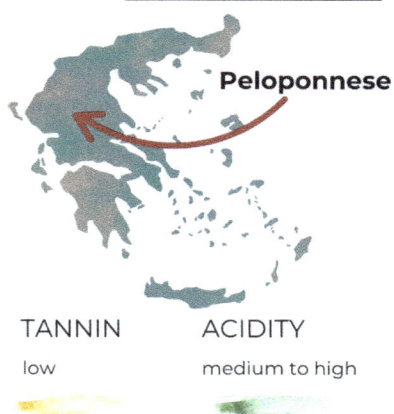

Peloponnese

PROFILE

FRUIT	BODY	TANNIN	ACIDITY
high	medium	low	medium to high

AROMAS

green apple

pear

bergamot

citrus blossom

jasmine

green tea

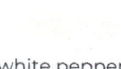

white pepper

vanilla

Sklava / Σκλάβα

One of Greece's oldest varieties, Sklava (**sklah**-vah) was once co-planted with Agiorgitiko around Peloponnesian vineyards. Today, it is bottled exclusively by Zacharias Vineyards.

In the vineyard, Sklava is drought resistant and seems quite happy in infertile soils. The wine shows a botanical character with herbs and tea along with notes of flowers, tree and stone fruit, and more exotic citrus fruits such as kumquat and bergamot. Medium-bodied with a noticeable oily texture and refreshing acidity.

- **How it's made:** dry, single varietal wines
- **Where it's made:** there are currently no PDOs or PGIs for Skalva
- **Who makes it best:** Zacharias Vineyards
- **What to eat with it:** salads, pasta with light sauces, seafood, chicken, white cheeses, savory tarts

Tachtas / Ταχτάς

Pronunciation: tahkh-**tas**

DESCRIPTION

Rarely found, this native Cretan variety makes highly aromatic and fruity wines with friendly acidity.

ORIGIN

Crete

PROFILE

FRUIT	BODY	TANNIN	ACIDITY
high	medium	low	medium

AROMAS

pear

peach

apricot

white flowers

Tachtas / Ταχτάς

Tachtas (tahkh-**tas**) is an old Cretan grape used largely for table wine and raisins. Not until Douloufakis Winery has it entered the quality wine sphere.

The origin of the grape's name has several stories. One being that it comes from the Turkish word tahta meaning "wood" or "board" due to the hardness of the vine stems, or possibly from the Turkish word taht meaning "throne" as an indication of the grape's quality. A third origin story is related to a Greek lullaby called tachtarisma.

A productive vine, Tachtas grapes are large and oblong, very pale green, and grow in large cylindrical bunches. It is sensitive to drought, hot winds, and powdery mildew.

Its wines are medium-bodied with lively acidity and aromatic with pears, stone fruits, and flowers.

- **How it's made:** dry, white wine
- **Where it's made:** P.G.I. Crete
- **Who makes it best:** Douloufakis Winery
- **What to eat with it:** fatty fish, poultry, lemon dressings/sauces, white pastas

Thrapsathiri / Θραψαθήρι

Pronunciation: thrap-sah-**thee**-ree

DESCRIPTION

Thrapsathiri wines are medium to full-bodied and textured with fresh acidity. Wines are moderately aromatic with predominate stone and tropical fruit notes.

ORIGIN

Crete

PROFILE

FRUIT	BODY	TANNIN	ACIDITY
high	medium to full	low	medium

AROMAS

peach

tropical fruits

melon

floral

mineral

Thrapsathiri / Θραψαθήρι

Yet another emerging grape from Crete, Thrapsathiri (thrap-sah-**thee**-ree) lived for years in the shadow of more popular Vilana and Vidiano. However, like Dafni and Plytó, Thrapsathiri is gaining ground. Literally, as plantings increase across the island.

The grape is highly resistant to drought, therefore does very well in the warmest and driest areas of Crete. While it grows all over Crete (and to a lesser extent in the Cyclades and Dodecanese), it prefers light calcareous soils. This has the advantage of controlling the vine's natural vigor and high yields which winemakers need to carefully manage to produce concentrated fruit. Thrapsathiri has good resistance to downy mildew but is susceptible to powdery mildew and botrytis bunch rot. It ripens in late August and you will find vines both bush and w re-trained.

Thrapsathiri wines are vivacious with pale lemon-lime in color and a fruit-forward aroma profile dominated by melon, peach, and tropical fruits. Generally on the full-bodied side with higher alcohol and fresh acidity, Thrapsathiri takes well to oak. Wines are at their best in their first few years but do gain more complexity and texture in those three - four years making it worth hanging onto one that long.

- **How it's made:** dry white wines, dry white blends. sweet white blends
- **Where it's made:** P.D.O. Sitia, P.D.O. Handakas Candia, P.D.O. Malvasia Sitia, P.D.O. Malvasia Handakas Candia, P.G.I Crete
- **Who makes it best:** Economou, Idai Gi, Th{eros} Wines Collectiva, Lyrarakis
- **What to eat with it:** herby baked chicken, pork with lemon, fish, seafood, saganaki, white cheeses (soft and hard), spanakopita

Tsaoussi / Τσαούση

Pronunciation: (**tsow**-see)

DESCRIPTION

Often blended with higher acidity grapes, Tsaoussi wines are fresh and fruity and also make successful skin contact wines.

ORIGIN

Ionian Islands

PROFILE

FRUIT	BODY	TANNIN	ACIDITY
medium to high	medium to high	low to medium	low to medium

AROMAS

melon

peach

apricot

grapefruit

quince

lemon zest

honey

aromatic herbs

Tsaoussi / Τσαούση

Grown mostly in the Ionian Islands, particularly Cephalonia, Tsaoussi (**tsow**-see) vines can also be found scattered across the north of Greece. A mixed-use variety, Tsaoussi is also consumed as a table grape.

An old variety, DNA analyses conducted in 2013 showed that it likely is a cross between the white Korithi Aspro and the black Mavrodaphne grapes. It grows in traditional, tall bush vines with large grapes susceptible to powdery mildew. Tsaoussi grapes have low to medium at best acidity and are often blended with higher acidity varieties like Robola or Sauvignon Blanc.

Not meant for extensive aging, Tsaoussi produces fresh and fruity wines with stone fruit, melon, citrus, and honey aromas. Some wineries on Cephalonia are also experimenting with extensive skin contact for this grape.

While 'Tsaoussi' is the most common moniker for this grape, you may also see it under one of its many synonyms: Tsaousis, Tsaousia, Tsaousiko, Tsavro, Tsaouski, Tsiasous, Tsaous Ouzoumi, Aspro, Chaouch, Tchavouch, Gavus, and Panse de Constantinople.

- **How it's made:** dry white varietal and blend wines, skin contact/amber wine
- **Where it's made:** P.G.I. Slopes of Aenos
- **Who makes it best:** Gentilini Winery, Sarris Winery, Sclavos Wines
- **What to eat with it:** fatty fish, grilled chicken, white pasta, seafood

Vidiano / Βιδιανό

Pronunciation: vee-dee-ah-**no**

DESCRIPTION

Vidiano is a versatile grape creating wines that are linear and textured to aromatic and creamy.

ORIGIN

Crete

PROFILE

FRUIT	BODY	TANNIN	ACIDITY
medium to high	medium to full	medium	medium

AROMAS

lemon

bergamot

stone fruits

floral

aromatic herbs

mineral

Vidiano / Βιδιανό

From where it originates in Rethymno where old, own-rooted bush vines still exist, across the island and now elsewhere in Greece, Vidiano (vee-dee-ah-**no**) is a rising star.

Vidiano has large bunches with round, yellow-green, and thick-skinned berries. It's a vigorous variety that needs to be controlled, usually by planting in poor limestone soils. Drought resistant but affected by powdery mildew, leaf roll, and grape moths that love the grape's sweet and lightly tannic pulp. One more difficult aspect of Vidiano is the grape's uneven ripening, requiring winemakers to keep a close eye on the vineyards from mid August to early September for harvest.

Wines from Vidiano tend to be textural and mouth coating with medium to high alcohol and acidity and flavors of stone fruits, warm citrus, flowers, and aromatic herbs. Winemakers are exploring a number of different techniques with this grape including extended lees ageing, oak and amphora ageing, skin contact, and sparkling wine production. Simple wines will keep for a few years after harvest but more complex barrel-fermented or lees/barrel-aged versions you can hold for five to seven years.

- **How it's made:** dry white wines, white blends, sparkling, amber
- **Where it's made:** P.D.O. Handakas-Candia, P.G.I Crete, P.G.I. Heraklion
- **Who makes it best:** Hliana Malihin, Dourakis, Oenops, Alexakis, Douloufakis, Diamantakis, Digenakis, Gavalas, Idaia, Karavitakis, Klados, Lyrarakis, Miliarakis, Manousakis, Pateriannaki, Silva, Strataridakis, Zacharioudakis
- **What to eat with it:** seafood or charcoal grilled fishes, zucchini-based dishes, pork, poultry, white pastas, cheese pies, salads, white cheeses, risotto

Vilana / Βηλάνα

Pronunciation: vee-**lah**-nah

DESCRIPTION

Medium intense and fruity, Vilana wines tend to be medium to full-bodied with high alcohol and a creamy texture.

ORIGIN

Crete

PROFILE

FRUIT	BODY	TANNIN	ACIDITY
medium to high	light to medium	low	medium to high

AROMAS

lemon

peach

orange zest

pear

melon

floral

aromatic herbs

spice

Vilana / Βηλάνα

As much as Crete is dominated by red grapes, Vilana (vee-**lah**-nah) has been the island's key white variety.

This naturally high-yielding and high alcohol grape grows best on Crete's elevated slopes, both of which enable Vilana to retain a freshness that balances its high alcohol. It needs to be monitored carefully in the vineyard though as it is sensitive to mildews and botrytis.

While wines from Vilana can run a gamut in style from simple and refreshing to full-bodied and creamy, its hallmark aromas are medium intense and fruit-forward with orange or lemon zest, pears, peaches, melon, and floral notes with soft acidity.

Typically unoaked and meant for early consumption, Vilana wines are becoming more complex as winemakers experiment with single vineyard fermentations and barrel fermentation and/or ageing. The different PDO production areas also offer different styles so it's worth understanding what goes into those:

- P.D.O. Peza: 100% Vilana
- P.D.O. Sitia: 70% Vilana 30% Thrapsathiri
- P.D.O. Chandakas-Candia: min 85% Vilana

- **How it's made:** dry white wines, white blends
- **Where it's made:** P.D.O. Peza, P.D.O. Sitia, P.D.O. Chandakas-Candia, P.G.I. Crete
- **Who makes it best:** Dourakis Rizitis, Gavalas, Idaia, Zaharioudakis Codex, Lyrarakis Pyrovolikes, Michalakis, Douloufakis
- **What to eat with it:** seafood salad or pasta, roasted fish, poultry, soft white cheese

Vostilidi / Βοστυλίδι

Pronunciation: voe-stee-**lee**-dthee

DESCRIPTION

Also known as
Goustolidi, this grape
gives fruity and
structured wines with
bright acidity and
noticeable tannins.

ORIGIN

**Ionian
Islands**

PROFILE

FRUIT	BODY	TANNIN	ACIDITY
medium to high	medium to full	medium	medium to high

AROMAS

tropical fruit

orange

bergamot

peach

fig

honey

floral   jasmine

Vostilidi / Βοστυλίδι

Vostilidi (voe-stee-**lee**-dthee), or Goustolidi comes from the Ionian islands where production is centered on Cephalonia (Kefalonia) and Zakynthos, with limited plantings on Corfu and Ithaca, as well as in the Peloponnese.

Wines from Vostilidi are golden-green in color with aromas of citrus, stone, and tropical fruit, honey, and even figs. Wines tend to be powerful, tending toward full-bodied with tannic grip and refined acidity.

- **How it's made:** dry white wines, blends
- **Where it's made:** P.D.O. Plagies Ainou, P.G.I. Slopes of Ainos, P.G.I. Zakynthos, P.G.I. Verdea of Zakynthos
- **Who makes it best:** Foivos Papastratis, Haritatos, Sarris Winery, Domaine Sfyri, Sclavos Wines, Petrakopoulos Wines
- **What to eat with it:** seafood, lemony sauces, grilled fish, poultry, blue cheese

The Pink Grapes

The Pink Grapes

Moschofilero   72
Roditis   74
Sideritis   78

Moschofilero / Μοσχοφίλερο

Pronunciation: mos-koe-**fee**-leh-roe

DESCRIPTION

Despite its reddish/grayish hue, it is mostly used for the production of dry, highly aromatic white wines.

ORIGIN

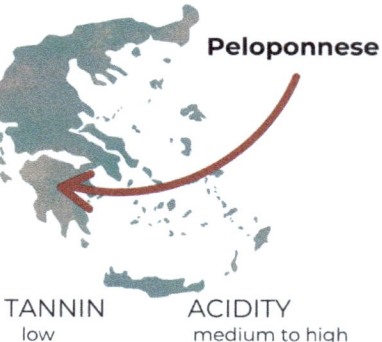

Peloponnese

PROFILE

FRUIT
medium

BODY
light to medium

TANNIN
low

ACIDITY
medium to high

AROMAS

citrus

stone fruits

orange zest

rose petals

lemon blossom

spice

Moschofilero / Μοσχοφίλερο

Native to the Peloponnesian Mantinia Plateau, Moschofilero (mos-koe-fee-leh-roe) is a late-ripening variety. While some old, goblet vines still exist, most plantings are trained on wires and need to be carefully pruned to the grape's vigor and high production. While resistant to powdery and downy mildew, it is susceptible to botrytis bunch rot. Bunches are medium to large in size, holding the medium-sized round, and thick-skinned pinkish grapes.

Yes! Despite most commonly being made into white wines, Moschofilero is a pink (or grey, as you like) colored grape. Increasingly popular though are also sparkling, rosé, oaked, and sweet wine styles.

An intensely aromatic variety, Moschofilero wines give a heady perfume of rose petals, lemon blossom, citrus, and spice. Wines tend to be crisp and fresh with lower alcohol. While most say wines should be drunk within the first four years after harvest, a few producers will argue that Moschofilero can age as much as 10 years or even more.

- **How it's made:** dry white wines, white blends, rosés, sparkling wines, sweet wines
- **Where it's made:** P.D.O. Mantinea, P.G.I. Arcadia, P.G.I. Peloponnese
- **Who makes it best:** Tselepos, Semeli, Skouras, Troupis, Bosinakis, Milia Riza, Moropoulos
- **What to eat with it:** white sauces, seafood, white poultry, (non spicy) Asian flavors, especially those with ginger-forward notes

Roditis / Ροδίτης

Pronunciation: roe-**dthee**-tees

DESCRIPTION

Previously used almost entirely for Retsina or "modest" wines, producers are now experimenting with higher quality Roditis wines.

ORIGIN

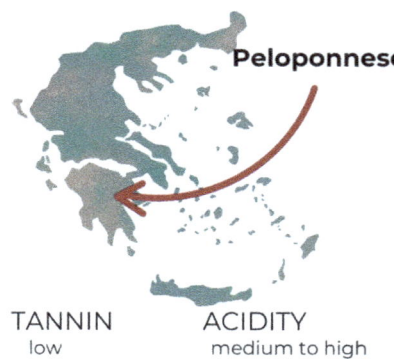

Peloponnese

PROFILE

FRUIT
medium to high

BODY
medium

TANNIN
low

ACIDITY
medium to high

AROMAS

green fruit

stone fruit

citrus

tropical fruit

herbaceous

mineral

Roditis / Ροδίτης

Together with Savatiano, Roditis (roe-**dthee**-tees) is one of the most planted varieties in Greece, making up nearly one-third of the country's total vineyard plantings. Despite how widely it is planted, it's likely not a grape you've thought about much.

For years, Roditis has been used as the base for nothing more than table wine which has led to it being overlooked by wineries and consumers alike. However, thanks to a handful of wineries making high-quality and interesting bottlings, Roditis is stepping into the spotlight.

One of Greece's neither white nor black varieties, Roditis grapes are medium to large-sized, round, and pinkish in color. Their moderately thick skins help with disease and drought resistance, but this late-ripening variety can be susceptible to downy mildew.

Grapes grown at higher altitudes give the most exciting wines, but much depends also on which clone is being used. There are currently eight Roditis clones and various biotypes being studied. Something complicated by the fact that solid and moisture conditions can alter appearance of the grapes, and that sometimes one might find vines with bunches made up of three different colors.

Particularly when grown at high altitude (700-1100 meters) or from old vines, Roditis can give bright, almost mineral wines with fresh acidity. Generally medium-bodied with lower to moderate alcohol. Roditis wines have lemony-citrus flavors often accompanied by green fruit or stone fruit.

Standard white wine fermentation in stainless steel tanks is still the most common winemaking method, but more producers are experimenting with lees ageing, oak ageing, and extended skin contact.

Unlike the well-known pink grape Moschofilero, Roditis has no anthocyanins, meaning that even extended skin contact will produce only a very pale amber color. As such, Roditis rosé wines do not exist (except in the possibility of a blend with a black grape).

While more complex Roditis wines may age for five to six years, most wines should be drunk within three years.

- **How it's made:** dry white wines, white blends, skin contact/amber wines, Retsina
- **Where it's made*:** P.D.O. Patras, P.D.O. Anchilaos, P.D.O. Slopes of Meliton, P.G.I. Magnesia, P.G.I. Ilia, P.G.I. Achaia, P.G.I. Attiki, P.G.I. Slopes of Aegialia
- **Who makes it best:** Rouvalis, Tetramythos Winery, Tatsis, Mercouri, Sant'Or, Acheon, Kanakaris Winery, Markogianni Winery, Mavrogianni Winery, Oenops, Papaioannou Winery
- **What to eat with it:** fried fish, pitas with spinach or cheese, snails

not an exhaustive list

Sideritis / Σιδερίτης

Pronunciation: see-dthe-**ree**-tees

DESCRIPTION

This rarer pink/grey variety creates crisp white wines with predominate citrus and floral aromas and an underlying spiciness.

ORIGIN

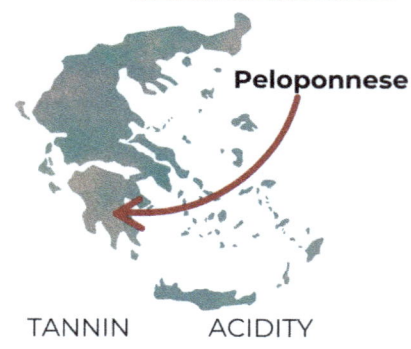

Peloponnese

PROFILE

FRUIT	BODY	TANNIN	ACIDITY
medium	medium	low	medium to high

AROMAS

citrus

green fruits

yellow fruits

peach

white flowers

white pepper

Sideritis / Σιδερίτης

Sideritis (see-dthe-**ree**-tees) is a pink-skinned grape that seems to just now be finding some popularity. From the northwest area of Peloponnese, it is also grown here and there in Attica and Evia. It is a vigorous variety producing large, pale pink berries on large bunches.

A late-ripening grape, sensitive to disease but drought resistant, its name comes from the Greek word for iron, *sidero*, because of the grape's tough skins.

Varietal wines from Sideritis (what few there are) are generally unoaked. Medium-bodied with fresh and lively acidity and moderate alcohol, Sideritis wines offer aromas of citrus, white flowers, green and yellow fruits, and spice.

- **How it's made:** dry white wines, white blends, Tsipouro
- **Where it's made:** P.G.I. Achaia, P.G.I. Peloponnese
- **Who makes it best:** Tetramythos Winery, Parparoussis Winery
- **What to eat with it:** seafood, light fish, lemon sauces, white cheeses, stuffed vine leaves, snails

The Black Grapes

The Black Grapes

Agiorgitiko	82
Avgoustiatis	84
Fokiano	86
Kotsifali	88
Liatiko	89
Limnio	94
Limniona	98
Mandilaria	100
Mavro Kalavrytino	104
Mavrodaphne	106
Mavrotragano	108
Mavroudi	110
Mouchtaro	112
Negoska	114
Romeiko	116
Vertzami	118
Vlahiko	120
Xinomavro	122

Agiorgitiko / Αγιωργίτικο

Pronunciation: eye-yore-**ree**-tee-koe

DESCRIPTION

Agiorgitiko makes fruity wines with high acidity and supple tannins. It makes refreshing rose wines but takes well to oak for a richer expression.

ORIGIN

Peloponnese

PROFILE

FRUIT	BODY	TANNIN	ACIDITY
high	medium to full	medium	medium to high

AROMAS

cherry

strawberry

raspberry

sweet spices

chocolate

purple flowers

red flowers

Agiorgitiko / Αγιωργίτικο

Agiorgitiko (eye-yore-**ree**-tee-koe) is the most common black grape in Greece. Nemea in the Peloponnese is its home and main PDO, as well as being the largest red wine appellation in Greece. It is not, however, the only place Agiorgitiko is grown. It can be found elsewhere in the Peloponnese as well as in Macedonia and Attika. Its name comes from Saint George, the original name for Ancient Nemea.

A late-ripening variety prone to fungal diseases, especially oidium, and very sensitive to leafroll virus, it produces thick bunches with medium-sized berries. Agiorgitiko performs better in poor soils, where its naturally high vigor can be controlled.

Agiorgitiko is used to produce a range of styles from young wines to complex oak aged examples, fruity rosés, and sweet wines. At its heart, its wines are juicy with supple tannins and a panoply of red fruit aromas, especially cherry and strawberry. These fresher wines should be drunk within the first few years after harvest. Careful oak ageing creates a deeper fruit profile along with sweet spices and chocolate and a more velvety tannin. These can be aged up to 10 years.

- **How it's made:** dry red wines, red blends, rosés, sweet wines, sparkling wines
- **Where it's made:** P.D.O. Nemea, P.G.I. Drama, P.G.I. Peloponnese
- **Who makes it best:** Akrathos, Athanasiou, Aivalis, Barafakas, Biblia Chora, Bizios, Bronovolias Estate, Gai'a, Gofas, Ieropoulos Family Wines, Lafkiotis, Lafazanis, La Tour Melas, Mitravelas, Monemvasia, Nemeion, Palivos, Papaioannou, Parparoussis, Pavlidis Estate, Pyrgakis, Rapti, Strofilia, Semeli, Skouras, Tetramythos Winery, Tselepos
- **What to eat with it:** burgers, moussaka, pizza, lasagna, tomato sauces, lamb, heavy/meatier fish, hard and semi-hard cheeses

Avgoustiatis / Αυγουστιάτης

Pronunciation: ahv-goose-tea-**ah**-tees

DESCRIPTION

With its full-body, velvety tannins, and vibrant acidity, Avgoustiatis wines are complex and rich in flavor.

ORIGIN

Ionian Islands

PROFILE

FRUIT	BODY	TANNIN	ACIDITY
medium	medium to full	medium	medium to high

AROMAS

cherry

strawberry

raspberry

blackberry

plum

cocoa

leather

brown spices

vanilla

hazelnut

Mediterranean herbs

Avgoustiatis / Αυγουστιάτης

While a lesser-known variety, Avgoustiatis (ahv-goose-tea-**ah**-tees) seems to be spreading far and wide. Hailing from the Ionian Islands, specifically Zakynthos, vines can be found in the Peloponnese, Attica, Crete, and Chios.

Known for its thick skins and deep color, Avgousitatis not only makes rich varietal wines, but is used to add color and complexity to red blends. Often softened with oak aging, its wines are deeply colored and full-bodied with velvety tannins, vibrant acidity, and a fulsome aroma profile including a panoply of red and black fruits, spices and herbs, leather, cocoa and more.

Because of its excellent structure, Avgoustiatis wines will age well and further develop in the bottle gaining more complexity.

- **How it's made:** dry red wines, red blends, rosé
- **Where it's made:** P.G.I. Ilia, P.G.I. Zakynthos
- **Who makes it best:** Brintzikis Estate, Ktima Grampsas, Mercuri Estate, Oenos Nature, Patriotis Winery, Stavropoulos Estate
- **What to eat with it:** roasted and grilled red meat, game, stifado/stews, hard cheese

Fokiano / Φωκιανό

Pronunciation: foe-kee-yah-**no**

DESCRIPTION

Fokiano offers fresh wines redolent of forest berries, spice, and aromatic shrubs to deeper, riper fruit flavors along with spice, and leather with age.

ORIGIN

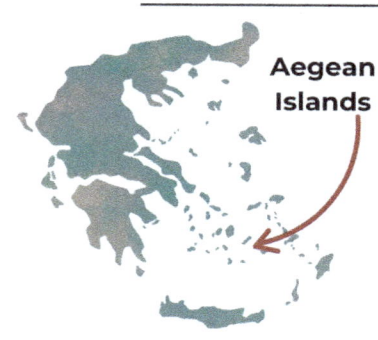

Aegean Islands

PROFILE

FRUIT	BODY	TANNIN	ACIDITY
medium	medium	low to medium	low to medium

AROMAS

cherry

backberry

forest fruit

red flowers

brown spice

white pepper

aromatic shrub

leather

Fokiano / Φωκιανό

Fokiano (foe-kee-yah-**no**) is most common to the Aegean and Cycladic Islands, especially Ikaria and Lipsi, with limited plantings on mainland Greece.

Fokiano also grows in Turkey's Aegean wine region under the name Foça Karası.

A moderately productive vine with medium-sized berries resistant to many fungal diseases and drought. Its wines are made into a range of styles from rosés to sweet wines with sun dried grapes.

In its youth, Fokiano is fresh and redolent with red fruit flavors like cherry, sour cherry, and berries. The red wines can and do evolve well in the bottle ripening with notes of dark fruit, spice, aromatic shrubs, and leather.

- **How it's made:** dry red wines, red blends, rosés, sweet wines, blanc de noir blends
- **Where it's made:** P.G.I. Aegean Sea, P.G.I. Ikaria, P.G.I. Cyclades
- **Who makes it best:** Afianes Wines, Karimalis Winery, Lipsi Winery, Ousyra Winery, Paradeisis Winery
- **What to eat with it:** stifado/stew, red meat stews, red sauces, hard yellow cheese

Kotsifali / Κοτσιφάλι

Pronunciation: côte-sih-**fah**-lee

DESCRIPTION

Kotsifali gives medium-bodied aromatic wines bursting with red fruits, sweet spices, and herbs, low tannin, and low moderate acidity.

ORIGIN

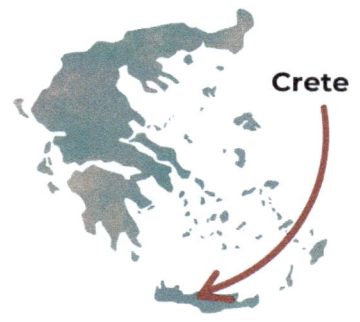

Crete

PROFILE

FRUIT	BODY	TANNIN	ACIDITY
high	medium	low	low to medium

AROMAS

cherry   strawberry   plum   blackfruits

sweet spices   herbal   earthy

Kotsifali / Κοτσιφάλι

One of the main Cretan grape varieties, Kostifali (côte-sih-**fah**-lee) is grown mainly around Heraklion and is practically synonymous with the island.

Kotsifali is a little tricky to work with in the vineyard. It is vigorous and highly productive and largely disease-resistant. All good things. But, it can be prone to downy mildew and botrytis. The main trick is to try to curb the grape's naturally high alcohol tendency but still leave it on the vine long for sufficient time to develop color and tannins.

While more and more producers are experimenting with single variety wines, Kotsifali is traditionally used as a blending partner with Mandalari or other black grapes, both Greek and international. This has been because, while intensely aromatic, Kotsifali wines tend to be high in alcohol but low in color, tannins, and acidity, and it often needs a more robust variety to create balance.

Kotsifali wines are redolent of red fruits such as cherry, plum, strawberry, sometimes even dried fruit, flowers, sweet spices, and Mediterranean herbs. Delicious with bright red fruit flavors in its youth, it also takes well to oak and oak aged examples can develop up to 10 years.

- **How it's made:** dry red wines, red blends
- **Where it's made:** P.D.O. Archanes, P.D.O. Peza, P.D.O. Candia, P.G.I. Crete, P.G.I. Heraklion
- **Who makes it best:** Karavitakis Winery, Lyrarakis Winery, Michalakis Wines, Zacharioudakis Winery, Zoumberakis Vineyards
- **What to eat with it:** charcuterie, rich meat dishes, casseroles, grilled meats

Liatiko / Λιάτικο

Pronunciation: lee-**ah**-tee-coe

DESCRIPTION

Liatiko makes pale colored wines with low tannins, soft acidity, and an earthy and aromatic bouquet of red fruits, flowers, and spice.

ORIGIN

Crete

PROFILE

FRUIT	BODY	TANNIN	ACIDITY
medium to high	medium to full	low to medium	medium

AROMAS

cherry

strawberry

red fruits

red flowers

spice

earthy

Liatiko / Λιάτικο

Found across the island, Liatiko (lee-**ah**-tee-coe) is considered a treasure of Crete. An ancient variety, Liatiko produces some of the island's highest quality red wines. Interestingly, it is one of the few varieties Greece and Turkey (knowingly) share and in Turkey, is grown in the inner Aegean region under the name Çal Karası.

Generally, Liatiko is a vigorous and productive variety resistant to both drought and diseases but susceptible to oidium. There's a great deal of clonal diversity with this grape which can be seen especially in the area of Sitia. Most of the vines here are old (35+ years) bush vines that are significantly less productive than vines elsewhere around Crete. It ripens early, taking its name from the Greek word for July which is often when it is harvested.

Despite having dark colored skins, Liatiko wines tend to be pale and more brick-garnet than ruby. Wines are highly aromatic with ripe red fruit, flowers, exotic spices, and a savory-earthiness. Low, soft tannins, often high alcohol, and moderate acidity combine to create a wine that Yiannis Karakasis MW describes as being "like a hug".

Liatiko wines take well to oak which contributes to its agability. Dry wines can develop well up to 10 years after harvest. The sun dried sweet versions can evolve for many decades more than that.

- **How it's made:** dry red wines, red blends, rosé, sweet wines
- **Where it's made:** P.D.O. Dafnes, P.D.O. Sitia, P.G.I. Crete
- **Who made it best:** Diamantakis, Douloufakis, Efrosyni, Idaia, Karavitakis, Lyrarakis
- **What to eat with it:** (dry wines) tomato-based dishes, grilled red meat, aged hard cheese, meaty fish (tuna, mackerel), even pizza and pasta; (sweet wines) blue cheeses, dried fruits, chocolate

Limnio / Λημνιό

Pronunciation: limb-nee-**yo**

DESCRIPTION

Distinctly herbal and savory, Limnio makes elegant wines with silky tannins.

ORIGIN

Aegean Islands Lemnos

PROFILE

FRUIT	BODY	TANNIN	ACIDITY
low to medium	medium	medium	medium

AROMAS

red berries

floral

sage

mint

thyme

Limnio / Λημνιό

Not to be confused with Limniona, Limnio (limb-nee-**yo**) is a grape of many names, known also as Lemnia, Limnia, Mavro Limino, Kalabaki, and Kalambak. Whichever name you use, drinking Limnio wines gives you a direct line to history. The grape rated mention by a number of Ancient Greek authors including Homer, Hesiod, and Polydefkis.

It is native to the Aegean island Lemnos (where it is often called Kalampaki), but most modern plantings are found in northern Greece. The vine is moderately vigorous and Limnio is quite a hardy grape, resistant to drought and most diseases (aside from downy mildew). It is adaptable and does well in most soil types. While it's relatively late-ripening, it does often present problems with even ripening, you might have bunches that contain a mix of berries from shriveled raisins to berries just reaching veraison.

Greece does light and medium-bodied red wines very well and Limnio is no exception. Its wines are largely aged in stainless steel but there are a few gently oaked examples hanging around and at least one producer is also experimenting with carbonic maceration. You will also frequently find it in blends or made into sweet wines (especially on Lemnos).

Varietal Limnio makes elegant wines with a silky texture with medium acidity and higher alcohol. Aromatic herbs often dominate and are accompanied by fresh red fruits. Generally ready to drink upon release, but can develop nicely for five to seven years in the bottle.

- **How it's made:** dry red wines, red bends, sweet wines
- **Where it's made:** P.D.O. Limnos, P.D.O. Slopes of Meliton, P.G.I. Avdira, P.G.I. Cyclades, P.G.I. Halkidiki, P.G.I. Ismaros
- **Who makes it best:** Anatolikos Vineyards, Domaine Kikones, Domaine Manalis Sikoinos, Domaine Porto Carras, Garalis Winery, Vourvoukeli Estate
- **What to eat with it:** meat dishes cooked with fruits or fruit sauces, charcuterie, meaty fish (tuna, mackerel), dark poultry meats

Limniona / Λημνιώνα

Pronunciation: limb-nee-**oh**-nah

DESCRIPTION

Powerful yet elegant,
Limniona wines have
soft tannins and
bright acidity with
red berry, floral, and
savory aromas.

ORIGIN

Thessaly

PROFILE

FRUIT	BODY	TANNIN	ACIDITY
low to medium	medium	medium	medium to high

AROMAS

strawberry

raspberry

violet

rose

herbal

sweet spices

pepper

Limniona / Λημνιώνα

Not to be confused with Lemnio, Limniona (limb-ree-**oh**-nah), also known as Lemniona, Limnionas, is a rising star thanks to the dedication of a handful of scientists, growers, and producers who have brought it back from the brink.

Originally from Thessaly, Limniona now appears in a number of places around Greece. It is a late-ripening and drought-resistant variety. While its thick skins provide some protection against oidium, due to the tightly-packed nature of the bunches, it is susceptible to downy mildew and botrytis. Growing it in areas with low rainfall helps both curb its natural vigor and decreases the chances of downy mildew and botrytis. In the realm of "not something you hear every day", Limniona is susceptible to sunburn. As such, growers need to ensure sufficient canopy protection during the growing season.

Maturation in oak barrels is common although some producers are also experimenting with other materials like clay. Wines have a vivid purple-red color and are both elegant and powerful with moderate alcohol, bright acidity, juicy tannins, and notes of herbs, flowers, red berries, pepper, and sweet spices.

Generally ready to drink upon release, most agree that it can be enjoyed up to five years after harvest, but some bottlings are still showing well at 10 years.

- **How it's made:** dry red wines, red blends, rosés, sparkling wine
- **Where it's made:** P.G.I. Meteora, P.G.I. Pieria, P.G.I. Tyrnavos
- **Who makes it best:** Christos Zafeirakis, Thanos Dougos, Nikos Karatzas, Monsieur Nicolas, Monemvasia Winery, Oenops, Karanika, Theopetra Estate, Tsililis, Wine Art Estate
- **What to eat with it:** dark poultry meat, rabbit, lamb, semi-hard and hard cow milk cheeses, grilled meats, mushrooms

Mandilaria / Μανδηλαριά

Pronunciation: mahn-dih-lar-ee-**ya**

DESCRIPTION

Mandilaria, or Mandilari, gives powerfully tannic wines with red and black fruit and earthy, leathery notes.

ORIGIN

Crete

PROFILE

FRUIT	BODY	TANNIN	ACIDITY
medium	light to medium	medium to high	medium to high

AROMAS

cherry

plum

black fruit

liquorice

leather

earthy

Mandilaria / Μανδηλαριά

Mandilaria (mahn-dih-lar-ee-**ya**) goes by many names including Amorgiano, Pariano, Vaftra, and Koundoura Black, but the most common alternative name is Mandilari, especially on Crete. Its origin is Crete, but it is also commonly found across the Aegean and Cycladic islands. On Crete, it is the most planted variety and takes a surprising second place (although by a large margin) to Assyrtiko on Santorini.

Both vigorous and productive, Mandilaria is prone to downy mildew and fungal diseases, particularly botrytis. Grapes grow in medium to large-sized bunches and have thick skins with high levels of tannin and anthocyanins, both of which contribute to the wine's grippy texture and deep color.

Despite the wine's deep color and hefty tannins, its wines are often more light-bodied with high acidity and low alcohol. It is therefore commonly blended with other grapes. Notably on Crete with Kotsifali and elsewhere with other native or international grapes. Mandilaria wines have a fruity-earthy character with aromas of cherries, plums, liquorice, and often leather.

Particularly varietal Mandilaria benefits from a few years of bottle ageing to tame the fearsome tannins but generally, due to its high acidity and tannin levels, Mandilaria can age well over eight to 10 years.

- **How it's made:** dry red wines, red blends, rosé, sweet wines (Vinsanto)
- **Where it's made:** P.D.O. Archanes, P.D.O. Candia, P.D.O. Dafnes, P.D.O. Peza, P.D.O. Rhodes, P.D.O. Sitia, P.G.I. Attiki, P.G.I. Crete, P.G.I. Cyclades, P.G.I. Heraklion
- **Who makes it best:** Aoton Winery, Diamantakis, Dourakis Winery, Idaia Winery, Lyrarakis, Michalakis Estate, Nikolou Winery, Vassaltis Vineyards, Venetsanos Winery,
- **What to eat with it:** lamb, roasted red meats, meaty fish like tuna, aged hard cheeses

Mavro Kalavrytino /
Μαύρο Καλαβρυτινό

Pronunciation: **mahv**-roe kah-lahv-rih-tee-**no**

DESCRIPTION

Medium-bodied with supple tannins and moderate acidity, Mavro Kalavrytino's wines show red and black fruits with spice and develop earthy and leather notes with age.

ORIGIN

Peloponnese

PROFILE

FRUIT	BODY	TANNIN	ACIDITY
medium to high	medium	medium	medium

AROMAS

strawberry

black fruits

red fruits

spice

earthy

leather

Mavro Kalavrytino / Μαύρο Καλαβρυτινό

Mavro Kalavrytino (**mahv**-roe kah-lahv-rih-tee-**no**), literally, 'Black of Kalavryta', grows specifically in the mountainsides of Ajialio and Kalavryta in the Achaia region, in the northwest part of the Peloponnese.

Nearly forgotten, it is thanks to concerted efforts by Panayiotis Papagiannopoulos from Tetramythos Winery that the grape has been saved.

A small, thin-skinned, and late-ripening grape, Mavro Kalavrytino created medium-bodied wines with supple tannins, and medium acidity. Its wines are fruity with aromas of both red and black fruits, subtle herbs and spice, and can develop leather and earth over time.

- **How it's made:** dry red wines, rosé
- **Who makes it best:** Tetramythos Winery
- **Where it's made:** P.G.I. Peloponnese
- **What to eat with it:** stuffed vegetables, grilled vegetables, red meat, dark poultry meat, mushrooms, charcuterie

Mavrodaphne / Μαυροδάφνη

Pronunciation: mah-vroe-**dhah**-fnee

DESCRIPTION

Famous for its sweet wines, Mavrodaphne creates elegant and savoury dry wines with black fruits, earthy, and herbal aromas.

ORIGIN

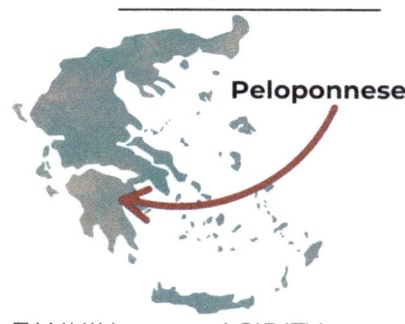

Peloponnese

PROFILE

FRUIT	BODY	TANNIN	ACIDITY
medium	medium to full	medium to high	medium

 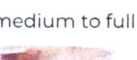 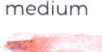

AROMAS

black cherry

plum

currant

black fruit

5 spice

laurel

sage

leather

Mavrodaphne / Μαυροδάφνη

Found primarily in the northwestern part of the Peloponnese and on Cephalonia, Mavrodaphne (mah-vroe-**dhah**-fnee) makes some of Greece's most notable sweet and fortified red wines.

Loose bunches and thick skins help protect the grape from botrytis and powdery mildew. It is, however, susceptible to downy mildew and dry conditions. This variety is also prone to millerandage (when bunches have berries of different sizes and maturity). It is a late-ripening variety, and requires a great deal of sunlight and heat in order to achieve ripeness.

Mavrodaphne's wines are distinctively nearly black in color with dense aromas, high alcohol, and medium acidity. Previously its wines were almost exclusively sweet, fortified or made with sun dried grapes. More recently, wineries are increasingly offering dry wines. Distinctive flavors of black cherry, currants, prune, Asian spices, laurel, and sage are often accompanied by a pleasant bitterness.

Dry wines can age for up to 10 years while sweet wines can live for decades.

- **How it's made:** dry red wines, red blends, sweet wines, rosé
- **Where it's made:** P.D.O. Mavrodaphne of Cephalonia, P.D.O. Mavrodaphne of Patra, P.G.I. Achaia, P.G.I. Ilia, P.G.I. Slopes of Aigialia, P.G.I. Slopes of Aenos
- **Who makes it best:** Achaia Clauss, Achaion, Foivos, Gentilini Winery, Haritatos, Markogiannis Winery, Mercouri Estate, Papargyriou, Parparoussis, Petrakopoulos Wines, Rouvalis Winery, Sant'Or Winery, Sarris, Sclavos, Tetramythos Winery, Zacharias
- **What to eat with it:** (dry) slow cooked lamb or pork, tomato sauces, sausages, mushrooms, savory tarts (sweet) chocolate-based desserts, dried fruits and nuts

Mavrotragano / Μαυροτράγανο

Pronunciation: mah-vroe-trah-**gah**-no

DESCRIPTION

Mavrotragano gives wines that are deep, full-bodied, tannic, and savory with touches of wild berries and mineral, often accompanied by flavors from oak ageing.

ORIGIN

Santorini

PROFILE

FRUIT	BODY	TANNIN	ACIDITY
medium	full	high	medium

AROMAS

wild berry

cherry

black fruit

blueberries

violet

spice

coffee

leather

mineral

Mavrotragano / Μαυροτράγανο

If you think island reds are light and fruity, you haven't experienced the deep, full-bodied, tannic, and savory wines from Mavrotragano (mah-vroe-**trah**-gah-no).

While grown on other islands and on the mainland, Mavrotragano traditionally grows on Santorini but plantings everywhere sustained big losses due to phylloxera. According to Yiannis Karakasis MW, even on Santorini Mavrotragano "... covers an estimated 14 hectares, or a bit more than 1% of the total vineyard area ...". It honestly doesn't sound like a fun grape to deal with so one can't really blame hesitant growers! A mid to late-ripening variety, Mavrotragano is not tolerant of dry conditions, is prone to millerandage (bunches containing a mix of ripe to overripe and not yet matured berries), and produces high inconsistent yields.

In the winery, oak is often employed to help soften the grape's naturally high and aggressive tannins. All the effort growers and winemakers go through is worth it for a sip of the wine's red fruits, wild berries, coffee, violet, spice, and mineral flavors.

High-end bottles benefit from at least four years bottle ageing and can develop well for several more years after that.

- **How it's made:** dry red wines, red blends, rosé
- **Where it's made:** P.G.I. Cyclades
- **Who makes it best:** Art Space Winery,Estate Argyros, Dougos Winery, Gavalas Estate, Domaine Gerovassiliou, Hatzidakis Winery, Karamolegos, Michailidi, Moschopolis, Nikolakis Vineyards, Pateromichelakis Winery, Domaine Sigalas, Santo Wines, T-Oinos, Vaptistis Winery, Vassaltis Vineyards, Volacus
- **What to eat with it:** roast beef, rib eye, game meat, moussaka, meatballs, roasted eggplant

Mavroudi / Μαυρούδι

Pronunciation: mahv-**roo**-dthee

DESCRIPTION

Mavroudi gives deeply colored and tannic wines with red and black fruit aromas complimented by cocoa and spice and with oak ageing coffee and vanilla.

ORIGIN

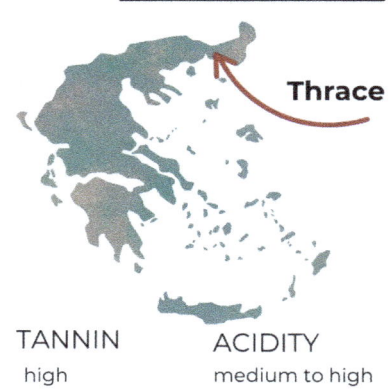

Thrace

PROFILE

FRUIT	BODY	TANNIN	ACIDITY
medium	medium	high	medium to high

AROMAS

black berry   sour cherry   red fruits   black fruits

cocoa   spice   coffee   tobacco   vanilla

Mavroudi / Μαυρούδι

One of the oldest Greek varieties, Mavroudi (mahv-**roo**-dthee) is mainly grown in Central Greece, the Peloponnese, and Thrace... Greek Thrace, Bulgarian Thrace, and Turkish Thrace. It's something of a tricksy grape, showing some differences in its DNA depending on where it's grown.

Mavroudi seems to be one of those grapes you really want to have to work with. The low-yielding vines produce small, darkly colored, and thick-skinned grapes that are susceptible to rot that ripen slowly. Its wines have firm acidity and pronounced tannins with aromas of blackberries, blueberries and sour cherries, with a medicinal-herbal character. Oak maturation can add spices, cocoa, coffee, leather, tobacco, and vanilla.

- **How it's made:** dry red wines, rosé, blends
- **Where it's made:** P.G.I. Epanomi, P.G.I. Ileia, P.G.I. Peloponnese
- **Who makes it best:** Anatolikos Vineyards, Domaine Gerovassiliou, Markogiannis Winery, Monemvasia Winery, Parparoussis Winery, Vourvoukeli Winery
- **What to eat with it:** red meats, game meats and birds, sausages, mushrooms, and hard cheeses

Mouchtaro /Μούχταρο

Pronunciation: **mookh**-tah-roe

DESCRIPTION

Mouchtaro's rich wines are characterized by concentrated flavors of red and black fruits, spice, and earthy notes.

ORIGIN

Central Greece

PROFILE

FRUIT	BODY	TANNIN	ACIDITY
medium	medium to full	medium	medium

AROMAS

red fruit

black fruit

herbal

sweet spices

chocolate

vanilla

earthy

Mouchtaro / Μούχταρο

Mouchtaro (**mookh**-tah-roe) is not going to be the first red wine on (almost) anyone's wine list, but it's a rising star in the couple few places that carry it.

In a country with rare varieties, Mouchtaro is a very rare variety. It hails from the Askri Valley outside Thebes where old bush vines produce naturally low yields of dark-skinned, medium-sized grapes. Its innate ability to withstand heat and drought conditions make this a promising grape for Central Greek wineries looking to mitigate the impact of climate change on their portfolio.

Mouchtaro wines are concentrated and complex with medium to high acidity and velvety tannins. The deeply colored wines offer aromas of black fruits, spices, herbs, with earthy undertones. Oak ageing can add nutty, chocolate, and vanilla flavors.

- **How it's made:** dry red wine, rosé, semi-sparkling, Tsipouro
- **Where it grows:** P.G.I. Sterea Ellada, P.G.I. Thiva
- **Who makes it best:** Knack Project, Muses Estate
- **What to eat with it:** red meats, sausages, aged hard cheese

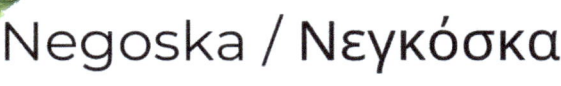

Negoska / Νεγκόσκα

Pronunciation: neh-**goe**-skah

DESCRIPTION

Marked by fresh acidity and notes of berries, black fruit, tomato, and earthy notes, varietal Negoska wines are hard to find but worth the hunt.

ORIGIN

Macedonia

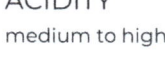

PROFILE

FRUIT
medium

BODY
medium to full

TANNIN
medium

ACIDITY
medium to high

AROMAS

berries

black fruit

tomato

leather

tobacco

Negoska / Νεγκόσκα

Negoska (neh-**goe**-skah) takes its name from its hometown Naoussa - albeit a Slavic derivative thereof. It's not the first grape people associate with Naoussa though, that honor would go to Xinomavro with which Negoska is commonly blended.

While originally from Naoussa, the grape has spread more widely across northern Greece throughout the appellations of Macedonia and Goumenissa. In Goumenissa, Negoska makes up at least 20% of the PDO wines, blended with Xinomavro. Varietal Negoska wines are few but on the rise, as people become won over by the grape's elegance. Varietal wines are rich with dark fruit and earthy flavors and soft tannins and acidity.

- **How it's made:** dry red wines, red blends, rosé, semi-sparkling
- **Where it's made:** P.D.O. Goumenissa, P.G.I. Macedonia, P.G.I Pella, P.G.I. Slopes of Paiko
- **Who makes it best:** Alexandride Estate, Chatzavaritis Estate, Katogi Averoff, Domaine Tatsis
- **What to eat with it:** stifado/stews, Moroccan lamb and tagine, moussaka, pastitsio, spaghetti bolognaise. savory tarts, charcuterie, yellow cheese

Romeiko / Ρωμέικο

Pronunciation: roe-**mey**-ee-coe

DESCRIPTION

While a red grape, modern Romeiko wines are more often made as blanc de noir wines with tree fruit, tropical, citrus, and sweet almond notes.

ORIGIN

Crete

PROFILE

FRUIT	BODY	TANNIN	ACIDITY
high	light to medium	low	high

AROMAS

sour cherry

blueberry

apple

pear

tropical fruit

orange marmalade

lemon

sweet almond

Romeiko / Ρωμέϊκο

With all the grapes coming out of Crete, Romeiko (roe-**mey**-ee-coe) is the only one native to western Crete in the region of Chania. Despite being a truly ancient grape, it is not particularly known off, or even on Crete.

The reason for its unpopularity lies in how misunderstood the grape is. Romeiko is a difficult grape to work with and it has only been recently that winemakers have learned how to harness it. People can be forgiven for dismissing it in the past as nothing better than a table wine or using it to create Marouvas, a rustic sherry-like wine.

While highly resistant to rot, due to its loose bunches that allow breezes to pass through the grapes, this late-ripening variety presents other problems. Even when fully ripe, bunches contain green, black, and pale pink berries, leading to high alcohol and acidity, but low color and tannins. Generally meaning that making a decent red wine with it is nearly impossible. Enter the modern Cretan winemakers who have unlocked the grape's potential by making refreshing rosé wines and crisp blanc de noir white wines.

- **How it's made:** dry blanc de noir wines, sparkling wine, rosé, dry red wines, red blends, sun dried sweet wines
- **Where it's made:** there are as yet no specific PDOs or PGIs for Romeiko
- **Who makes it best:** Dourakis Winery, Karavitakis Winery, Manousakis Winery, Pateromichelakis Winery
- **What to eat with it:** white meat poultry, pork, spanakopita, white sauces, creamy risottos

Vertzami / Βερτζάμι

Pronunciation: ver-**tza**-mee

DESCRIPTION

Vertzami is a relatively rare grape that gives big, savory wines with dark fruit and herbal aromas with high alcohol and big tannins.

ORIGIN

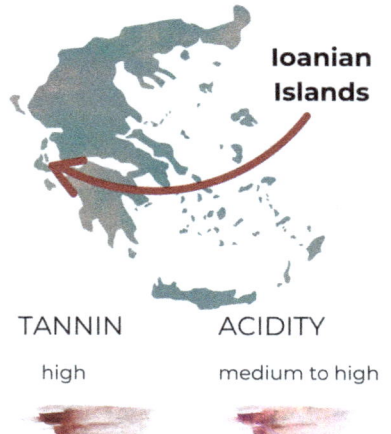

Ioanian Islands

PROFILE

FRUIT	BODY	TANNIN	ACIDITY
medium	full	high	medium to high

AROMAS

red fruits

red & black currants

plum

violet

tobacco

eucalyptus

savory

cedar

chocolate

Vertzami / Βερτζάμι

If you thought Cabernet Sauvignon had already hoarded all the anthocyanins to produce its deeply colored and tannic wines, then you haven't met Vertzami (ver-**tza**-mee) yet.

Found mainly on the Ionian islands Lefkada and Corfu, Vertzami has also been making a name for itself in the western Peloponnese, Central Greece, and Eprus. Regardless of where it grows, Vertzami prefers to live in lower altitude sites with poor/infertile soils and low water stress. It is largely resistant to diseases but needs a good deal of warmth to fully ripen, which is why it doesn't do as well at higher, cooler locations.

While often found in blends, varietal Vertzami wines do exist. They're so deeply colored as to be almost black, have moderate to high alcohol, firm acidity, and generous tannins. Big aromas, often oak influenced, display laurel, eucalyptus, cedar, cinnamon, black fruits, and berries.

Wines often want at least some bottle ageing and can develop beautifully over a decade or even more.

- **How it's made:** dry red wines, red blends
- **Where it's made:** P.G.I. Lefkada
- **Who makes it best:** Antonopoulos Vineyards, Markogianni Winery, Karanikos Winery, Lefkaditiki Gi Winery, Siflogo Winery
- **What to eat with it:** red meats, stifado/stew, lasagna, tomato sauces

Vlahiko / Βλάχικο

Pronunciation: **vlah**-hee-coe

DESCRIPTION

Vlahiko wines have firm acidity and fine tannins with marked pepper spice and red and black fruit and earthy notes.

ORIGIN

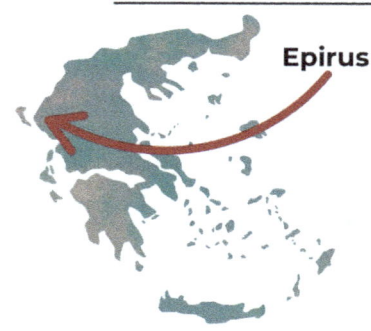

Epirus

PROFILE

FRUIT	BODY	TANNIN	ACIDITY
medium	medium	low to medium	medium to high

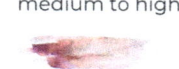

AROMAS

red berry

black currant

blueberries

herbal

forest floor

black pepper

earthy

mineral

Vlahiko / Βλάχικο

Hailing from Epirus, Vlahiko (**vlah**-hee-kce), also commonly spelled Vlachiko or Blachik are frequently blended with other local grapes, particularly Bekari and Debina. However, some producers are bottling beautiful examples of varieta wines.

Grown in one of the coldest parts of northwestern Greece, near the Albanian border, Vlahiko displays all the joys of a cool climate red wine. Wines have relatively low alcohol, unsurprising given how cold their vineyards are, high acidity, and fine tannins. Fresh red and blue berry fruit aromas mingle with spices and pepper. The wine's light structure makes it a perfect antidote for those tired of over extracted, over oaked, heavy red wines. It's also a great summer red wine as its refreshing personality does well lightly chilled.

Contrary to the thought that a red wine has to be tannic and oaky to age well, Vlahiko can develop well in the bottle for as much as seven years.

- **How it's made:** dry red wines, red blends, rosé (blends), sparkling
- **Where it's made:** P.G.I. Ioannina
- **Who makes it best:** Domaine Glinavos, Jima Winery, Katogi Averoff, Zoinos Winery
- **What to eat with it:** charcuterie, red meat, game birds, stuffed vegetables but especially peppers, aged cheeses

Xinomavro/Ξινόμαυρο

Pronunciation: ksee-**no**-mav-row

DESCRIPTION

Possibly Greece's greatest red wine, Xinomvro has high acidity and a dense tannic structure hidden in a deceptively pale color.

ORIGIN

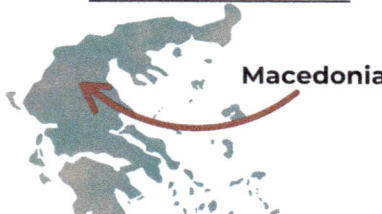

Macedonia

PROFILE

FRUIT	BODY	TANNIN	ACIDITY
medium to high	medium to full	high	high

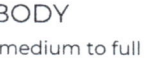

AROMAS

cherry

strawberry

raspberry

prune

tomato

olive

brown spices

tobacco

vegetal

earthy

Xinomavro / Ξινόμαυρο

While not Greece's most widely planted black grape, Xinomavro (ksee-**no**-mav-row) is undoubtedly its King. Originally from Naoussa in Macedonia, Xinomavro is widely planted across Greece and can be found in everything from varietal red to blanc de noir traditional method sparkling wines.

As high in the instep as you would expect a king to be, Xinomavro is both finicky and demanding in the vineyard. It demands a specific terroir, and its tight bunches are sensitive to water stress, powdery and downy mildew, and botrytis. A late-ripening variety, it requires careful cultivation to ensure low, healthy yields.

When everything goes well in the vineyard and winery, Xinomavro gives stunning, elegant wines with structure, firm tannins, bright acidity, and a flavor profile that gains increasing complexity as it ages. From red fruits, flowers, tomatoes, olives, thyme, and spices to tobacco, nuts, dried tomatoes, and mushrooms with age.

Most Xinomavro (red) wines need at least a few years bottle ageing, particularly those from Naoussa that benefit from at least four years; but wines can easily age 20 or more years.

- **How it's made:** blanc de noir, dry red wines, red blends, rosé, sparkling wines
- **Where it's made:** P.D.O. Naoussa, P.D.O. Amynteo, P.D.O. Goumenissa, P.D.O. Rapsani, P.G.I. Florina, P.G.I. Macedonia, P.G.I. Opountia Lokridos, P.G.I. Pella, P.G.I. Plagies Paikou, P.G.I. Velventos*
- **Who makes it best:** Alpha Estate, Boutari, Chatzivaritis, Dalamara, Diamantis, Dougos, Foundi, Karanika, Karydas, Katagi Averoff, Kir Yianni, Ktima Ligas, Oenops Wines, Pegasus, Domaine Tatsis, Thymiopoulos, Tsantali
- **What to eat with it:** lamb, grilled or braised red meats, tomato sauces, rich and aged cheeses, charcuterie

Part 2
Greece's Wine
Regions

Greece has nine wine regions spread across the mainland and its islands. And while not every prefecture or island has a robust wine industry, many areas are home to significant grape growing and production.

Greece is mountainous but at the same time has many plains and valleys. Both the mainland and the islands are affected by sea influences and soil types vary around the country. All these influences create a vast array of meso and micro climates that affect wine production in each area. For example, Assyrtiko from Santorini is a completely different animal than Assyrtiko from Achaia.

Speaking of Santorini and Achaia, you will find many designations included on Greek wine labels. The specific designations for each region are listed in the region sections, but broadly, classifications are:

- Protected Designation of Origin (P.D.O.) / Προστατευμένη Ονομασία Προέλευσης (Π.Ο.Π.)
- Protected Geographical Indication (P.G.I.) / Προστατευόμενη Γεωγραφική Ένδειξη (Π.Γ.Ε.)

Aegean Islands

Region At a Glance: Aegean Islands

The wine world contains many fascinating and even unique terroir. Given their proximity to water, exposure to the elements, and the very manner in which they are created, islands tend to be among the most fascinating. Greece is home to more islands than any other wine producing country. Its Aegean islands, with their complex blend of soils, volcanic origins, strong, often violent winds, and bounty of rare grapes offers some of the country's most distinctive wines.

Greece has no fewer than 6000 islands! Although less than 250 are inhabited. So, when we talk about the Aegean islands, which do we mean? They are*: Agathonisi, Amorgos, Anafi, Andros, Antiparos, Astypelea, Chios, Crete, Delos, Ikaria, Ios, Kalymnos, Karpathos, Kasos, Kea, Kos, Kythos, Lemnos, Leros, Lipsi, Milos, Mykonos, Naxos, Nikia, Paros, Patmos, Rhodes, Samos, Santorini, Serifos, Sikinos, Symi, Syros, Thirasia, Tilos, Tinos which are further broken down into the Cycladic and Dodecanese islands:

- **Cyclades:** Amorgos, Anafi, Andros, Antiparos, Delos, Ios, Kea, Kythos, Milos, Mykonos, Naxos, Paros, Santorini, Serifos, Sikinos, Syros, Thirasia, Tinos,
- **Dodecanese:** Agathonisi, Astypelea, Ikaria, Kalymnos, Karpathos, Kasos, Kos, Leros, Lipsi, Nikia, Patmos, Rhodes, Symi, Tilos

Crete's wine industry is so robust as to be its own region and is addressed separately.

No two of the Aegean islands are the same, but we can speak in broad terms about the climatic and soil conditions, as well as viticultural practices throughout.

Generally the Aegean Islands have a typical Mediterranean climate with hot, dry summers and mild winters. The rainy period usually lasts from November through March although the amount of rain each island gets varies greatly. For example, Santorini and Thirasia have a more semi-arid climate with very limited amounts of rainfall. Given their general amount of exposure, islands tend to be windy which, to a degree, helps keep vineyards healthy. However, strong winds, such as the northern meltemia which particularly plague the Cycladic islands, can be violent and cause massive vineyard damage in the spring.

Soil composition across the islands varies but for the most part, they all share a barren quality and minimal water resources. The mixture of infertile soils include limestone (Lemnos); granite (Tinos and Samos); calcareous, sandy, or sandy-clay (Paros), and famously, volcanic (especially Santorini and Thirasia).

Viticulture on the islands is old and, as some of the islands escaped the plague of phylloxera, the vines themselves are often ancient and own-rooted. Many vines, therefore, still grow in traditional head-trained bushes. Notable exceptions include Santorini with its famous kouloura "basket" vines and the kladeftiko "ring" vines. Paros employs an entirely different method. Here, old bush vines grow freely creating a floor covering of vines locally known as apoltaries. Mechanization is not possible in most vineyards, particularly on those where terraces (pezoules) have been built to counter soil erosion and retain the precious little rainwater.

The islands are rich in native grapes, both white and red, but with many being rare and used in few wineries. International grapes play a much smaller role in winemaking. The most common international grape used, especially on Samos, is Muscat of Alexandria.

Native Grapes Include:

- **White:** Aidani, Assyrtiko, Athiri, Begleri, Gaiduria, Katsano, Maloukato, Monemvasia, Potamisi, Serfiotiko
- **Red:** Augustiatis, Chidiriotiko, Fokiano, Koumari, Limnio, Mandilaria, Mavrotragano, Rozaki

Despite the small size of the individual Aegean Islands, they produce significant quantities of wine and at great quality. There are, therefore, a number of Protected Designation of Origin (PDO) and Protected Geographical Indication (PGI) labels you might encounter.

- **PDOs:**
  - PDO Limnos (Lemnos) (ΠΟΠ Λήμνος)
    - Still white: dry, demi-dry, semi-sweet (Muscat Blanc); still dry red (Limnio); naturally sweet and fortified red
  - PDO Malvasia Paros (ΠΟΠ Malvasia Πάρος)
    - Still white; naturally sweet; fortified sweet (Monemvasia min 85%; Assyrtiko)
  - PDO Muscat of Limnos (ΠΟΠ Μοσχάτος Λήμνου)
    - Still naturally sweet, fortified sweet white (Muscat of Alexandria)
  - PDO Muscat of Rodos (ΠΟΠ Μοσχάτος Ρόδου)
    - Naturally sweet; fortified sweet
  - PDO Paros (ΠΟΠ Πάρος)
    - Still white (Monemvasia); still red (Monemvasia 66%, Mandilaria 33%)
  - PDO Rodos (ΠΟΠ Ρόδος)
    - Still white: dry, semi-dry, semi-sweet; sparkling white (all sweetness levels); still rosé: dry, semi-dry, semi-sweet; sparkling rosé (all sweetness levels); still red: dry, semi-dry, semi-sweet
  - PDO Samos (ΠΟΠ Σάμος)
    - Still naturally sweet, fortified sweet (Muscat Blanc)

- PDO Santorini (ΠΟΠ Σαντορίνη)
  - Still white; dry; naturally sweet; fortified sweet; sweet (Assyrtiko; Aidani, Athiri)

- **PGIs:**
  - PGI Aegean Sea (ΠΓΕ Αιγαίο Πέλαγος)
    - Still white, rosé, and red; fortified white; seni-sparkling and sparkling white and rosé
  - PGI Chios (ΠΓΕ Χίος)
    - Still white and red
  - PGI Cyclades (ΠΓΕ Κυκλάδες)
    - Still white, rosé, and red; fortified white and red
  - PGI Dodekanese (ΠΓΕ Δωδεκανήσου)
    - Still white; still dry red
  - PGI Ikaria (ΠΓΕ Ικαρία)
    - Still white, rosé, and red
  - PGI Kos (ΠΓΕ Κώς)
    - Still white, rosé, and red
  - PGI Lesvos (ΠΓΕ Λέσβος)
    - Still white, rosé, and red
  - PGI Slopes of Ampelos (ΠΓΕ Πλαγιές Αμπέλου)
    - Still white
  - PGI Thapsana (ΠΓΕ Θαψανά)
    - Still white and red

Recommended Producers:

Tinos: T-Oinos, Vaptistis Winery, Volacus
Paros: Moraitis Winery
Santorini: Argyros, Gai'a, Gavalas, Hatzidakis, Karamolegos, Santo Wines, Sigalas, Vassaltis, Venetsantos
Rhodes: Cair
Samos: Nopera Wines, United Winemaking Agricultural Cooperative of Samos
Lemnos: Garalis Winery
Lipsi: Lipsi Winery
Ikaria: Afianes Wines, Ikaria Winery

Central Greece

Region At a Glance: Central Greece / Sterea Ellada

Central Greece, or Sterea Ellada, borders the Ionian Sea to the west, Epirus and Thessaly to the north, the Aegean Sea to the east, and to the south the Corinthian Gulf. This is Greece's most heavily populated region, especially as it encompasses Athens, as well as being one of the most heavily planted regions with almost 30% of the county's vineyards. Like its neighbors Epirus and Thessaly, Central Greece encompasses part of the Pindos Mountains, making this one of the country's most mountainous areas.

Between its size and varied topography, Central Greece has a wide diversity of soil and mesoclimates. In the west with the sea influence, it is humid and rainy, with the mountainous center being cold and drier, leading to the warmest and driest area in the east, giving each of the four sub-zones a particular character.

- **Fthiotida** sits in the north of Central Greece, close to Thessaly and has a mild climate due to daytime sea breezes and cool air coming from Mount Parnassos. Cabernet Sauvignon is the most promising variety here.
- **Viotia** to the southeast includes the plain of Thebes where Savatiano and Roditis grow in deep, limey-clay soils. At the border with Attica on the slopes of Mount Kitheronas, native and international grapes grow and where some producers are currently working to revive the red Mouchtaro grape.

In the southeast, surrounded on three sides by water, is mountainous **Attika**, home to Athens. The driest and warmest area of Central Greece, annual precipitation usually measures no more than 482 mm (19 in), with summer temperatures soaring above 40 C (104 F), and where massive fires plague the area.

133

Soils here are mainly calcareous with sandy loam and infertile, especially suitable for Savatiano, cultivated in densely planted, goblet-trained vineyards. native varieties tend to mirror those on the nearby Cycladic islands.

- **Evia** in the east is Greece's largest island after Crete. Hills and mountains here alternate with low fields and plans. The coolest area is in the islands north whereas the south is hot, dry, and extremely windy. While international grapes are common here, native varieties tend to mirror those on the nearby Cycladic islands.

Grapes Varieties Include:

Native grapes:
- **White:** Assyrtiko, Aidani, Athiri, Malagousia, Roditis, Savatiano
- **Red:** Agiorgitiko, Limnio, Mandalaria, Vradiano

International grapes: Cabernet Franc, Cabernet Sauvignon, Carignan, Chardonnay, Gewürztraminer, Grenache, Malvazia, Merlot, Sauvignon Blanc, Syrah

Central Greece currently has no Protected Designation of Origin (PDO) but, with such a large amount of land given over to vines, it's little wonder that there are an equally large number of Protected Geographical Indication (PGI) labels.

- **PGIs**
  - PGI Anavyssos (ΠΓΕ Ανάβυσσος)
    - Still white
  - PGI Atalanti Valley (ΠΓΕ Κοιλάδα Αταλάντης)
    - Still white, rosé, and red
  - PGI Attiki (ΠΓΕ Αττική)
    - Still white, rosé, and red; fortified white and red

- PGI Evia (ΠΓΕ Εύβοια)
  - Still white, rosé, and red
- PGI Fthiotida (ΠΓΕ Φθιώτιδα)
  - Still white, rosé, and red
- PGI Gerania (ΠΓΕ Γεράνια)
  - Still white, rosé, and red
- PGI Ilion (ΠΓΕ Ίλιον)
  - Still white
- PGI Karystos (ΠΓΕ Κάρυστος)
  - Still white, rosé, and red
- PGI Lilantio Pedio (ΠΓΕ Ληλάντιο Πεδίο)
  - Still white, rosé, and red
- PGI Markopoulo (ΠΓΕ Μαρκόπουλο)
  - Still white
- PGI Martino (ΠΓΕ Μαρτίνο)
  - Still white, rosé, and red
- PGI Opountia Locris (ΠΓΕ Οπούντια Λοκρίδα)
  - Still white, rosé, and red
- PGI Pallini (ΠΓΕ Παλλήνη)
  - Still white
- PGI Parnassos (ΠΓΕ Παρνασσός)
  - Still white, rosé, and red
- PGI Retsina of Attiki (ΠΓΕ Ρετσίνα Αττικής)
- PGI Retsina of Koropi (Attiki) – ΠΓΕ Ρετσίνα Κορωπίου (Αττικής)
- PGI Retsina of Markopoulo (Attiki) – ΠΓΕ Ρετσίνα Μαρκοπούλου (Αττικής)
- PGI Retsina of Megara (Attiki) – ΠΓΕ Ρετσίνα Μεγάρων (Αττικής)
- PGI Retsina of Mesogeia (Attiki) – ΠΓΕ Ρετσίνα Μεσογείων (Αττικής)
- PGI Retsina of Paiania (Attiki) – ΠΓΕ Ρετσίνα Παιανίας (Αττικής)
- PGI Retsina of Pallini (Attiki) – ΠΓΕ Ρετσίνα Παλλήνης
- PGI Retsina of Pikermi (Attiki) – ΠΓΕ Ρετσίνα Πικερμίου (Αττικής)

- PGI Retsina of Spata (Attiki) – ΠΓΕ Ρετσίνα Σπάτων (Αττικής)
- PGI Retsina of Evia (ΠΓΕ Ρετσίνα Ευβοίας)
- PGI Retsina of Halkida (Evoia) – ΠΓΕ Ρετσίνα Χαλκίδας (Ευβοίας)
- PGI Retsina of Gialtra (ΠΓΕ Ρετσίνα Γιάλτρων)
- PGI Retsina of Karystos (ΠΓΕ Ρετσίνα Καρύστου)
- PGI Retsina of Viotia (ΠΓΕ Ρετσίνα Βοιωτίας)
- PGI Retsina of Thebes Voiotias (ΠΓΕ Ρετσίνα Θήβας)
- PGI Ritsona (ΠΓΕ Ριτσώνα)
- PGI Slopes of Kithaironas (ΠΓΕ Πλαγιές Κιθαιρώνα)
  - Still white, rosé, and red
- PGI Slopes of Knimida (ΠΓΕ Πλαγιές Κνημίδας)
  - Still white, rosé, and red
- PGI Slopes of Parnitha (ΠΓΕ Πλαγιές Πάρνηθας)
  - Still white, rosé, and red
- PGI Slopes of Pendeliko (ΠΓΕ Πλαγιές Πεντελικού)
  - Still white
- PGI Sterea Ellada (ΠΓΕ Στερεά Ελλάδα)
  - Still white, rosé, and red; fortified white and red
- PGI Spata (ΠΓΕ Σπάτα)
  - Still white
- PGI Thiva (ΠΓΕ Θήβα)
  - Still white, rosé, and red

Recommended Producers:

Fthiotida: Argyriou Winery, Ktima Hatzimichalis, Ktima Karadimos
Viotia: Akriotou Microwinery, Muses Estate
Attika: Anastasia Fragou Winery, Ktima Evharis, Ktima Matsa, Ktima Papagiannakos, Ktima Vassiliou, Mylonas Winery
Evia: Avantis Estate, Vriniotis Winery

Crete

Region At a Glance: Crete

Crete, Greece's largest island, is also one of its most significant and prolific wine regions. With a large number of not only native but endemic grapes and complex topography, Crete is one of the leaders in Greece's wine future.

While the majority of vineyards are located on the eastern side of the island, grapes grow across Crete, especially in the north where they benefit from north and northeasterly sea winds. Lowlands and plateau-top plains, some topping out at 1,000 meters (3,300 feet) make up most of the island. From west to east are the Lefka Ori, Idi, and Dikty mountain ranges which form plateaus and gorges. Soils are largely clay and limestone. Crete is a sunny, hot, and dry island. Little rainfall occurs during the summer months, usually only around 50 mm (2 in). The extreme heat is mitigated by sea winds and those high elevations.

Crete has four distinct sub-regions. From west to east they are: Chania, Rethymno, Heraklion, and Lasithi.

- **Chania** in the west is dominated by the Lefka Ori mountain range. Between its heights and the clouds that roll off the Mediterranean, Chania is both the coolest and most humid region in Crete. This is also the main place for the up-and-coming Romeiko grape.
- **Rethymno** lies between Chania and Heraklion, bordered to the north and south, respectively, by the Cretan and Libyan Seas. The Lefka Ori range spills over from Chania into Rethymno's west and Mount Psiloritis dominates the east, creating a largely mountainous terrain. While this is the least developed winegrowing region of Crete, it has the honor of being the birthplace of the island's premier white grape, Vidiano.

- Making up the center of the island is **Heraklion** (or Iraklio) so large and prolific that it has three of its own sub-regions: Peza, Archanes, and Daphnes. The vineyards of Peza stretch across both hilly terrain and the plain of Peza at altitudes of up to 700 meters (2,300 feet). The region's deep calcareous soils are mostly given over to Vilana, Kotsifali, and Mandilaria. The vineyards of Archanes sit more or less in the center of Crete, just south of the city of Heraklion. Its limey-clayey soils host mostly Kotsifali, at altitudes ranging from 300 to 400 meters (1,000-1,300 feet). On the northeastern slopes of Mount Idi, at 300 to 490 meters (1,000-1,600 feet) are the vineyards of Dafnes. This is home to Liatiko, Greece's 5th most planted grape, which grows in the sandy, often gravelly and infertile soils.
- The majority of **Lasithi** vineyards lay in the northeast, in Sitia, home to one of Greece's oldest winemaking areas. The area is rich innative grapes including Liatiko and Mandilaria which occupy lower altitudes on the Mount Orno foothills along the Cretan Sea coastline; as well as Vilana and Thrapsathiri which primarily grow farther south at altitudes of 1,000 meters (3,300 feet) on the Ziros plateau.

While most of Crete's vineyards are modern and vines trained on wires, there are still pockets of old goblet vines across the island. A number of international grapes have done well on Crete, but the island contributes a huge variety of native grapes to Greece, many of which grow only on Crete.

Grape Varieties Include:

Native grapes:
- **White:** Assyrtiko, Dafni, Dermatas, Melissaki, Plyto, Tachtas, Thrapsathiri, Valaitis, Vidiano, Vilana
- **Red:** Kotsifali, Liatiko, Mandilari(a), Romeiko, Tsardana, Xinomavro

International grapes: Cabernet Sauvignon, Chardonnay, Grenache, Malvasia di Candia, Mourvedre, Muscat of Spinas, Roussanne, Sangiovese, Syrah, Viognier

Given how prolific the island's wine industry is, there are several Protected Designation of Origin (PDO) and Protected Geographical Indication (PGI) labels you might encounter.

- **PDOs:**
  - PDO Archanes (ΠΟΠ Αρχάνες)
    - Still dry red (Kotsifali, Mandilaria)
  - PDO Dafnes (ΠΟΠ Δαφνές)
    - Still dry red; sweet (Liatiko)
  - PDO Handakas – Candia (ΠΟΠ Χάνδακας-Candia)
    - Still dry white (Vilana must be min 80%; Vidiano, Assyrtiko, Athiri, Thrapsathiri) and red (Kotsifali must be min 70%; Mandilaria)
  - PDO Malvasia Handakas-Candia (ΠΟΠ Malvasia Χάνδακας-Candia)
    - Still white; sweet white (Assyrtiko, Athiri, Vidiano, Thrapsathiri, Muscat Blanc, Muscat di Candia Aromatica; Liatiko)
  - PDO Malvasia Sitia (ΠΟΠ Malvasia Σητείας)
    - Still white; naturally sweet; fortified sweet (Assyrtiko, Athiri, Vidiano, Thrapsathiri, Muscat Blanc, Muscat di Candia Aromatica; Liatiko)
  - PDO Peza (ΠΟΠ Πεζά)
    - Still dry white (Vilana) and red (Kotsifali, Mandalaria)
  - PDO Sitia (ΠΟΠ Σητεία)
    - Still white (Vilana min 70%; Thrapsathiri); dry still red; naturally sweet; fortified sweet (Liatiko 80%, Mandilaria 20%)

- **PGIs:**
  - PGI Chania (ΠΓΕ Χανιά)
    - Still white, rosé, and red; fortified white and red
  - PGI Crete (ΠΓΕ Κρήτη)
    - Still white, rosé, and red
  - PGI Iraklio (Heraklion) (ΠΓΕ Ηράκλειο)
    - Still white, rosé, and red
  - PGI Kissamos (ΠΓΕ Κίσσαμος)
    - Still white, rosé, and red
  - PGI Lasithi (ΠΓΕ Λασίθι)
    - Still white, rosé, and red
  - PGI Rethymno (ΠΓΕ Ρέθυμνο)
    - Still white, rosé, and red; fortified white and red

Recommended Producers:

Chania: Dourakis Winery, Manousakis Winery, Pateromichelakis Winery
Heraklion: Diamantakis Winery, Douloufakis Winery, Idaia Winery, Lyrarakis Winery, Silva Daskalaki Winery, Thalassinos Microwinery, Theros Wines Collectiva, Zacharioudakis Winery

Epirus

Region At a Glance: Epirus

Epirus in northwest Greece is one of the country's smallest regions (islands aside). It is bordered by Albania to the north, the Ionian Sea in the west, Macedonia to the northeast, Thessaly to the southeast, and Central Greece to the south.

In terms of production quantities, Epius produces significantly more than the county's other regions. Despite that, it is an exciting wine region with distinct native grapes, quality wine, and one of the few with a sparkling wine tradition. Made mostly with the white Debina grape, but Epirus also produces rosé bubbles and styles range from cheap carbonated wines to pét-nat, and traditional method wines. Small as it is, Epirus' largest production area is Ioannina, especially Zitsa (also the region's only PDO) and Metsovo.

Epirus is largely mountainous with an average altitude of 700 meters (2,300 feet). At a glance, the high altitude may seem too cold for grapes, but the Ionian Sea to the west moderates summer heat and winter cold. The Pindos Mountain range along the Albanian border forms a natural barrier against strong northern winds while also contributing to rainfall levels throughout Epirus.

Vineyards cover both steeply sloped hillsides, where soils are sandy loam, as well as carpet the richer clay soils of lower-lying plains. The majority of vines grow in wire-trained trellises, but there are still some older goblet-pruned Debina bush vines peppered throughout the vineyards of Zitsa.

While international grapes have found a foothold here, Epirus's most exciting wines come from native grapes, many of which are specific only to this region.

Grape Varieties Include:

Native grapes:
- **White:** Debina, Malagousia, Roditis
- **Red:** Agiorgitiko, Bekari, Vlahiko, Xinomavro

International grapes: Cabernet Franc, Cabernet Sauvignon, Merlot, Muscat of Alexandria, Pinot Noir, Traminer

The region's smaller wine production does not indicate a lower quality of wine and Epirus has one Protected Designation of Origin (PDO) and several Protected Geographical Indication (PGI) labels you might encounter.

- **PDOs:**
  - PDO Zitsa (ΠΟΠ Ζίτσα)
    - Still, dry white; sparkling, dry and semi-sweet white
- **PGIs:**
  - PGI Epirus (ΠΓΕ Ήπειρος)
    - Still white, rosé, and red; semi-sparkling and sparkling white; semi-sparkling rosé
  - PGI Ioannina (ΠΓΕ Ιωάννινα)
    - Still white, rosé, and red; semi-sparkling and sparkling white; semi-sparkling rosé
  - PGI Metsovo (ΠΓΕ Μέτσοβο)
    - Still white and red

Recommended Producers:

Katogi Averoff, Ktima Glivanos, Jima Winery, Zoinos Winery

Ionian Islands

Region at a Glance: Ionian Islands

The Ionian Islands, Greece's most easterly region, include seven islands (from north to south): Corfu, Paxos, Antipaxos, Lefkada, Ithaca, Cephalonia, and Zakynthos.

The island group lacks extremes but the maritime influence here is obvious. The Pindos Mountains on the mainland create a natural barrier influencing rainfall and winds with the islands receiving some of the highest levels of rainfall in all of Greece. Additionally, humidity levels here are higher than elsewhere in the country. A few islands even record precipitation levels through humidity accumulation vs rainfall. Aside from Paxos and Antipaxos, the islands are quite mountainous, a wide variety of soil types and mesoclimates affecting viticulture.

The majority of viticultural interest is focused on just four of the islands: Corfu, Lefkada, Cephalonia, and Zakynthos.

- The largest of the Ionian Islands, **Corfu** is shielded from weather extremes by the Pantokratoras Mountain in the north. Red grapes, like Petrokorithos, grow in the heavy soils on the mountain's slopes while white grapes, predominantly Kakotrygis, grow in the coarser soils of the southern plains. More than any other island is humidity a problem on Corfu.
- Unlike the other islands, **Lefkada** is given over almost entirely to one grape: Vertzami. The island's proximity to the Greek mainland has a profound effect on the island with cold winds from the Pindos Mountains.
- **Cephalonia** (or Kefalonia) stands as the Ionian Island group's leading wine producer in terms of both fame and quality. Varied soil types include limestone around Mount Ainos, with sandy patches in the southwest and heavier clay elsewhere.

In particular the calcareous limestone soils which lend the island's famed Robola of Cephalonia its distinct minerality. Humidity here is a problem, causing a number of fungal diseases and mildew problems, particularly as most of the Robola plantings   are bush vines which don't allow for a lot of airflow.

- **Zakynthos** is the warmest of the Ionian Islands and has a higher percentage of low-lying flat lands vs mountains. Here the soils tend to be heavier and more fertile. Zakynthos is the birthplace of the Traditional Designation Verdea but also devotes a fair amount of production to the red Avgoustiatis.

Grape Varieties Include:

While there are a few international grapes, notably Muscat Blanc, grown in the islands, the majority of viticulture is given over to native Greek varieties.

Native grapes
- **White:** Goustolidi, Kakotrtigis, Lagorthi, Malacousia, Migdali, Moschatella, Pavlos, Robola, Roditis, Skiadopoulou, Thiatiko White, Tsaousi
- **Red:** Araklinos, Avgoustiatis, Glikopati, Katsakoulias, Korfiatis, Mavrodaphne, Mavrothiatiko, Petrokorintho, Vertzami

The Ionian Islands have three Protected Designation of Origin (PDO) zones, all on Cephalonia, and a number of Protected Geographical Indication (PGI) labels across the other islands.

- **PDOs:**
  - PDO Mavrodaphne of Kefalonia (ΠΟΠ Μαυροδάφνη Κεφαλληνίας)
    - Still, dry red and naturally sweet red from Mavrodaphne

147

- PDO Muscat of Kefalonia (ΠΟΠ Μοσχάτος Κεφαλληνίας)
    - Still, naturally sweet, fortified sweet, and sweet from Muscat Blanc
- PDO Robola of Kefalonia (ΠΟΠ Ρομπόλα Κεφαλληνίας)
    - Still, dry white from Robola

- **PGIs:**
    - PGI Corfu (ΠΓΕ Κέρκυρα)
        - Still white
    - PGI Halikouna (ΠΓΕ Χαλικούνα)
        - Still white
    - PGI Lefkada (ΠΓΕ Λευκάδα)
        - Still white, rosé, and red
    - PGI Mantzavinata (ΠΓΕ Μαντζαβινάτα)
        - Still white, rosé, and red
    - PGI Metaxata (ΠΓΕ Μεταξάτα)
        - Still red
    - PGI Slopes of Ainos (ΠΓΕ Πλαγιές Αίνου)
        - Still white, rosé, and red; semi-sparkling
    - PGI Verdea of Zakynthos (ΠΓΕ Βερντέα Ονομασία Κατά Παράδοση Ζακύνθου)
        - Still white with Skiadopoulo making up at least 50%
    - PGI Zakynthos (ΠΓΕ Ζάκυνθος)
        - Still white, rosé, and red

Recommended Producers:

Corfu: Grammenos Winery, Pontiglio Winery
Cephalonia: Gentilini Winery, Ktima Foivos. Sclavos Wines
Zakynthos: Ktima Grampsa

Macedonia

Region At a Glance: Macedonia

Together with Thrace, Macedonia marches along the northernmost part of Greece. While the Aegean Sea occupies most of its southern border along with Thessaly, the rest of the region is surrounded by land with Epirus to the southwest, Albania to the northwest, Northern Macedonia and Bulgaria to the north, and Thrace to the east.

Macedonia has a variable climate and is typically flatter than one finds in the south of Greece with ample rainfall and largely fertile soils. For this reason, agriculture is a major source of income to this part of the country which, aside from Thessaloniki, sees significantly less tourism than other regions. Vineyards, orchards, and other crops benefit from a Mediterranean influence from the sea and regional lakes. Here you will find a variety of native and international grapes, but the undisputed king here is Xinomavro.

The region is home to a number of sub-regions which are, from east to west: Florina, Imathia, Kilkis, Piera, Thessaloniki, Serres, Halkidiki, Drama, and Kavala.

- With its more continental climate, **Florina** is the coldest viticultural area of Greece and home to one of the country's one of the most important viticultural areas: The Plateau of Amynteo. Unlike the rest of largely flat Macedonia, Florina is semi-mountainous with altitudes exceeding 500-700 meters (1640-2300 feet), but the area's four lake's help temper the cold. The vineyards of Amynteo lie between the Vermio and Voras massifs and Xinomavro dominates plantings. Soils here contain thick alluvial deposits and are generally sandy, warm, and of low fertility.
- While Florina has rightly earned prestige through its Amynteon wines, Naoussa in **Imathia** is arguably Greece's greatest red wine producing region, dedicated to dry, red wines from Xinomavro.

Vineyards run along the foothills and eastern slopes of Mount Vermio at 100-400 meters (328-1310 feet) in varied soils which range from acid schist to high concentrations of lime and clay. Xinomavro ripens late here, increasing its vulnerability to late season cold and rain.

- Like much of Macedonia, **Kilkis** is given over mostly to Xinomavro plantings which have easier conditions here than Imathia's Naoussa. What marks this subregion is the semi-mountainous PDO zone of Goumenissa where the local red variety Negoska comprises 23-30% of the total cultivation.

- Located in the southern part of central Macedonia, **Pieria** hosts Macedonia's newest wine scene. With significant influences from the Thermaic Gulf and Aliakmonas and Pinios rivers, combined with the Olympus, Pieria, and Titaros mountain ranges, this up and coming region is creating promising wines with native and international varieties.

- Located in central Macedonia, **Thessaloniki** with its Mediterranean climate has become a significant wine producing region. Hot summers and mild winters, tempered by sea breezes, combined with proximity to the Thermaikos and Strymonikos gulfs, lakes Koronia and Volvia, and the Chortiatis, Sivri, and Vertiskos mountains create ideal conditions for growing grapes.

- Despite having the Kerkini-Vertiskos-Kerdylion mountains to the west and the Orvilos-Menioi-Pangaio mountains to the east, **Serres** is a relatively flat region. It has a long history of ouzo production and recently is coming into its own for wine production.

- **Halkidiki** is most characterized by the poor soils and steep terrain of its vineyards on the slopes of Mount Meliton. While a number of varieties, native and international alike, have done well here, the grape that has thrived the most has been the white Malagousia.

- Assyrtiko and international red varieties fare well in **Drama**'s warmth and dryness.

- **Kavala**, temperate, humid, and hilly, lies between the coast and Mount Pangeon. Its deep and fertile soil have given a home to a number of international white grapes.

Grape Varieties Include:

Native grapes

White: Asproudes, Assyrtiko, Malagousia, Roditis
Red: Koniaros, Limnio, Mavrodaphne, Moschomavro, Negoska, Nigrikiotiko, Sklithro, Xinomavro

International grapes: Cabernet Franc, Cabernet Sauvignon, Chardonnay, Gewürztraminer, Grenache, Merlot, Pinot Noir, Sauvignon Blanc, Semillon, Ugni Blanc

A large production zone, Macedonia is home to four PDOs and a large number of PGIs.

- **PDOs:**
  - PDO Amyndeon (ΠΟΠ Αμύνταιο)
    - Still rosé: dry or semi-dry; sparkling rosé: dry or semi-dry; still red: dry, semi-dry, semi-sweet (Xinomavro)
  - PDO Goumenissa (ΠΟΠ Γουμένισσα)
    - Still, dry red (Negoska, Xinomavro)
  - PDO Naoussa (ΠΟΠ Νάουσα)
    - Still red: dry, semi-dry, semi sweet (Xinomavro)
  - PDO Slopes of Meliton (ΠΟΠ Πλαγιές Μελίτωνα)
    - Still white and red

- **PGIs:**
  - PGI Agora (ΠΓΕ Αγορά)
    - Still white, rosé, and red

- PGI Drama (ΠΓΕ Δράμα)
  - Still white, rosé, and red
- PGI Epanomi (ΠΓΕ Επανομή)
  - Still white and red
- PGI Florina (ΠΓΕ Φλώρινα)
  - Still white, rosé, and red; semi-sparkling white
- PGI Grevena (ΠΓΕ Γρεβενά)
  - Still rosé and red
- PGI Halkidiki (ΠΓΕ Χαλκιδική)
  - Still white, rosé, red
- PGI Imathia (ΠΓΕ Ημαθία)
  - Still white, rosé, and red
- PGI Kastoria (ΠΓΕ Καστοριά)
  - Still white, rosé, and red
- PGI Kavala (ΠΓΕ Καβάλα)
  - Still white, rosé, and red
- PGI Kozani (ΠΓΕ Κοζάνη)
- PGI Macedonia (ΠΓΕ Μακεδονία)
  - Still, semi-sparkling, fortified white, rosé, and red
- PGI Mount Athos (ΠΓΕ Άγιο Όρος)
  - Still white, rosé, red; fortified red
- PGI Nea Mesimvria (ΠΓΕ Νέα Μεσημβρία)
  - Still white and red
- PGI Pangeon (ΠΓΕ Παγγαίο)
  - Still white, rosé, and red
- PGI Pella (ΠΓΕ Πέλλα)
  - Still white, rosé, and red
- PGI Pieria (ΠΓΕ Πιερία)
  - Still white, rosé, and red; fortified white and red
- PGI Serres (ΠΓΕ Σέρρες)
  - Still white, rosé, and red
- PGI Siatista (ΠΓΕ Σιάτιστα)
  - Still white, rosé, and red; naturally sweet white and red
- PGI Sithonia (ΠΓΕ Σιθωνία)
  - Still white and red
-

- PGI Slopes of Paiko (ΠΓΕ Πλαγιές Πάικου)
  - Still white, rosé, and red
- PGI Slopes of Vertiskos (ΠΓΕ Πλαγιές Βερτίσκου)
  - Still white, rosé, and red
- PGI Thasos (ΠΓΕ Θάσος)
  - Still white, rosé, and red
- PGI Thessaloniki (ΠΓΕ Θεσσαλονίκη)
  - Still white, rosé, red
- PGI Velvento (ΠΓΕ Βελβεντό)
  - Still white, rosé, and red

Recommended Producers:

Florina: Ktima Alpha, Ktima Karanika, Ktima Kir-Yianni
Kozani: Diamantis Winery,Ktima Voyatz
Imathia: Boutari, Ktima Chrisohoou, Ktima Kir-Yianni, Thymiopoulos Wines
Pella: Ktima Ligas
Pieria: Chatzivarities, Ktima Tatsis
Thessaloniki: Ktima Gerovassiliou
Halkidiki: Domaine Porto Carras, Tsantali
Serres: Domaine Nerantzi, Ktima Biblia Chora
Drama: Costa Lazatidi, Chateau Nico Lazardi, Ktima Pavlidis, Wine Art Estate

Peloponnese

Region At a Glance: The Peloponnese

At the southernmost point of the Balkan Peninsula is the Peloponnese. While the Peloponnese has seven sub-regions, including Corinth, Argolida, Arcadia, Laconia, Achaia, Ilia, and Messina, it has two main growing regions. The first, encompassing the central and northern areas, include the region's most famous PDOs: Mentinia and Nemea. Stretching from Mount Panachaiko to the Ionian coast and down to Messina in the west is the second main vine growing area including Achaia, Ilia, and Messina.

While largely Mediterranean in climate, mountain slopes, altitude, and proximity to the sea creates a myriad of meso and micro climates. Most vineyards sit on rugged terrain or plateau of the mountainous and semi-mountainous region receiving protection through various mountain ranges from cold winds. The region is marked by mild winters (although snow does happen in the north of the Peloponnese), short springs, hot and dry summers, and long autumns.

- **Corinth** is something of a contradiction as a wine region. On the one hand, PDO Nemea produces some of Greece's most lauded red wines, while on the other, it also pumps out huge quantities of mass-produced wine. The vineyards of Nemea, planted with Agiorgitiko, form the largest PDO in the country and are spread across the flats around Nemea (260-350 meters / 850-1150 feet); the the semi-mountainous zone (350-600 meters / 1150-1970 feet) in the west; and the mountain zone (600-800 meters / 1950-2625 feet) at the foot of Mount Kyllini. At lower altitude, soils are largely alluvial, becoming coarser and more calcareous and gravel-based at higher altitudes.

- South of Corinth is **Argolida**. With similar soil and climate to Corinth, and holding 7% of PDO Nemea vineyards, Argolida is very much an extension of Corinth.
- In the heart of the Peloponnese, surrounded by tall mountains, sits **Arcadia**. Distinguished from the rest of the region by its lower humidity and temperatures and higher rainfall, both winter and summer are relatively mild. Due to the cooler temperatures, harvests here are among the latest in the whole region. Soils are clay, rocky, and poor in nutrients. Arcadia is home to Mantinia, whence hail some of the country's best Moschofilero wines. Old vineyards (40+ years old) are often densely planted goblet vines, dry-farmed in sandy loam soil, and very often organically farmed.
- While not as developed as elsewhere in the Peloponnese, **Laconia** is making a name for itself with the re-emergence of the Monemvasia grape, and with sweet wine production.
- **Achaia**, with its vineyards in Egialia and Patras, is one of the largest wine growing areas of Greece, in terms of both area and volume. In the north, the vineyards of Egialia lay along gentle slopes and area protected from cold sea breezes by the Gulf of Corinth. Sitting from 250 to 850 meters (820-2788 feet), soils range from white calcareous to fertile sandy loam. To the west on lower altitudes of 450 to 500 meters (1476-1640 feet) are the vineyards of Patras.
- **Ilia**'s vineyards grow in fertile soils on flatlands southeast of the mountains. Production is significantly smaller here with a broad preference for international varieties.
- The vineyards of **Messinia**, with a similar propensity for international grape varieties, sit on plateaus facing the Ionian Sea and are planted largely in calcareous soils.

Grape Varieties Include:

Native grapes
- **White:** Assyrtiko, Asproudi, Goustolidi, Kidonitsa, Malagousia, Monemvasia, Roditis, Savatiano, Tourkopoula, White Skilopnithis
- **Red:** Agiorgitiko, Avgustiatis, Corinthiaki, Fokiano, Mandilaria, Mavrodaphne, Mavrokalavrytino, Mavroudi, Red Skilopnithis, Smirneiko
- **Pink:** Moschofilero

International grapes: Cabernet Sauvignon, Chardonnay, Grenache Blanc and Rouge, Muscat, Refosco, Syrah, Tempranillo, Ugni Blanc

- **PDOs:**
  - PDO Mantinia (ΠΟΠ Μαντινεία)
    - Still white, sparkling white (min 85% Moschofilero with Asproudi)
  - PDO Mavrodaphni of Patra (ΠΟΠ Μαυροδάφνη Πατρών)
    - Still red, naturally sweet, fortified sweet (min 51% Mavrodaphne with Corinthiaki)
  - PDO Monemvasia – Malvasia (ΠΟΠ Μονεμβασία-Malvasia)
    - Still white: sweet, fortified (Min 51% Monemvasia with Assyrtiko, Kidonitsa, and Asproudi)
  - PDO Muscat of Patra (ΠΟΠ Μοσχάτο Πατρών)
    - Still white: naturally sweet, fortified sweet (Muscat Blanc)
  - PDO Muscat of Rio Patra (ΠΟΠ Μοσχάτος Ρίου Πάτρας)
    - Still white: naturally sweet, sweet, fortified sweet (Muscat Blanc)
  - PDO Nemea (ΠΟΠ Νεμέα)
    - Still red: dry, semi-sweet, sweet, fortified sweet (Agiorgitiko)

- PDO Patra (ΠΟΠ Πάτρα)
  - Still white: dry, semi-dry, semi-sweet (Roditis)

- **PGIs:**
  - PGI Achaia (ΠΓΕ Αχαΐα)
  - Still white, red, and rosé; semi-sparkling white and rosé
  - PGI Argolida (ΠΓΕ Αργολίδα)
  - Still white, red, and rosé
  -
  - PGI Arcadia (ΠΓΕ Αρκαδία)
    - Still white, red, and rosé; semi-sparkling white and rosé
  - PGI Ilia (ΠΓΕ Ηλεία)
    - Still white, red, and rosé
  - PGI Klimenti (ΠΓΕ Κλημέντι)
    - Still white, red, and rosé
  - PGI Korinthos/Corinth (ΠΓΕ Κόρινθος)
    - Still white, red, and rosé
  - PGI Laconia (ΠΓΕ Λακωνία)
    - Still white, red, and rosé
  - PGI Letrinoi (ΠΓΕ Λετρίνοι)
    - Still red
  - PGI Messinia (ΠΓΕ Μεσσηνία)
    - Still white and red
  - PGI Peloponnese (ΠΓΕ Πελοπόννησος)
    - Still white, red, and rosé
  - PGI Pisatis (ΠΓΕ Πισάτις)
    - Still white (Roditis)
  - PGI Pylia (ΠΓΕ Πυλία)
    - Still white
  - PGI Slopes of Aigialia (ΠΓΕ Πλαγιές Αιγιαλείας)
    - Still white, red, and rosé; semi-sparkling white and rosé
  - PGI Tegea (ΠΓΕ Τεγέα)
    - Still red
  - PGI Trifilia (ΠΓΕ Τριφυλία)
    - Still white, red, and rosé

Recommended Producers:

Corinth: Bairaktaris Estate, Barafakas Wines, Ktima Driopi, Gai'a Wines, Ieropoulous Family Winery & Vineyard, Ktima Semeli, Lafazanis Winery, Lantidis Vineyards, Papargyriou Winery, Zacharias Vineyards

Argolida: Koroniotis Winery, Ktima Skouras

Arcadia: Bosniakis Winery, Ktima Tselepos, Troup's Winery

Laconia: Monemvasia Winery, Vatistas Winery

Achaia: Achaia Clauss, Acheon Winery, Antonopoulos Vineyards, Rouvalis Winery, Tetramythos Wines

Ilia: Ktima Brintzikis, Ktima Mercouri, Markogianni Winery

Thessaly

Region At a Glance: Thessaly

Thessaly lies in the heart of mainland Greece. With an economy based more on grain and cotton than on grapes, it has nonetheless positioned itself as an important region for the young generation of winemakers. Mountain slopes with soils rich in organic matter and abundant water from several rivers have created a generous growing environment for Thessaly's five sub-regions: Larissa, Tyrnavos, Karditsa, Trikala, and Magnisia.

- Located in **Larissa** is the PDO Rapsani, not only the most important appellation of Thessaly, but the smallest area to cultivate Xinomavro (370 acres). Vineyards lay on semi and mountainous terrain on the eastern slopes of Mount Olympus, at altitudes ranging between 150 and 750 meters (492-2460 feet). Xinomavro, Krassato, and Stavrato goblet vines are joined by a number of trellised international varieties.
- More known for tsipouro than for wine, **Tyrnavos** is nonetheless known for making aromatic Roditis wines and for the red Limniona.
- **Karditsa**'s mild climate is home to a unique, regional grape, Messenikola Black (or Mavro Messenikola). Vineyards are planted in light and gravely soil on slopes as high as 700 meters (2296 feet). While newer plantings are trellised on wires, the majority of vines are trained in traditional goblets.
- On the Thessaly plain, surrounded by the Tzoumerka, Hasia, and Lakmos mountains is **Trikala**. More famous for the monasteries of Meteora than for wine, Trikala's winemaking efforts are being revived with a large focus on the red Limniona variety.
- **Magnesia**, situated on the coastal area overlooking the Pagasitikos Gulf in deep, limey-clay soils, Roditis vines flourish.

While newer plantings are trained on wires, most vines are older and trained into tall-trunk goblets. The Roditis clone grown is known as "green Roditis" and differs from clones elsewhere in Greece in that it does not acquire the variety's signature pinkish-grey hue.

Grape Varieties Include:

Native grapes
- **White:** Assyrtiko, Batiki, Roditis, Savatiano
- **Red:** Krasato, Limnio, Limniona, Mavro Messenikola, Stavrato, Xinomavro

International grapes: Cabernet Sauvignon, Carignan, Chardonnay, Muscat of Hamburg, Sauvignon Blanc, Syrah

While growing vines is not widely practiced in Thessaly, the area does have three important PDOs and several PGIs to look out for:

- **PDOs**
  - PDO Anchialos (ΠΟΠ Αγχίαλος)
    - Still dry white
  - PDO Mesenikola (ΠΟΠ Μεσενικόλα)
    - Still dry red (70% Mavro Messenikola 30% Carignan & Syrah)
  - PDO Rapsani (ΠΟΠ Ραψάνη)
    - Still, dry red (Krassato, Savrato, Xinomavro)

- **PGIs**
  - PGI Elassona (ΠΓΕ Ελασσόνα)
    - Still white, rosé, and red
  - PGI Karditsa (ΠΓΕ Καρδίτσα)
    - Still white, rosé, and red
  - PGI Krania (ΠΓΕ Κρανιά)
    - Still white and red

- PGI Krannona (ΠΓΕ Κραννώνα)
    - Still white, rosé, and red
- PGI Magnisia (ΠΓΕ Μαγνησία)
    - Still white, rosé, and red
- PGI Meteora (ΠΓΕ Μετέωρα)
    - Still white, rosé, and red; sparkling white and rosé
- PGI Thessalia (ΠΓΕ Θεσσαλία)
    - Still white, rosé, and red; semi-sparkling rosé; sparkling white and rosé
- PGI Tyrnavos (ΠΓΕ Τύρναβος)
    - Still white, rosé, and red

Recommended Producers:

Magnissa: Apostolaki Winery, Ktima Milea
Larissa: Dougos Winery, Ktima Karipidi, Ktima Katsaros, Ktima Zafeirakis, Tsantali
Trikala: Ktima Theopetra
Karditsa: Monsieur Nicolas Winery

Thrace

Region At a Glance: Thrace

Ancient Thrace was a center for those who worshipped at the altar of Dionysus. Now shared among Bulgaria, Greece, and Turkey, wine still plays a role in the region, if at a rather lessened level. Viticulture in Greek Thrace has significant ground to more profitable crops but is making a comeback.

Warm and humid, the Rodopi Mountains protect vineyards against cold northern winds while the region's proximity to the Aegean Sea moderates winter temperatures and helps keep temperatures cooler in the summer. Soil types vary widely across the small region, ranging from deep, sandy soils along the Aegean to gravely and less fertile soils on the slopes of the Rodopi Mountains. Thrace receives some of Greece's highest rainfall which can make it difficult for grapes to reach maturity. The exception being the coastal strip from Kavala to Maronia.

Grape Varieties Include:

Native grapes
- **White:** Assyrtiko, Athiri, Malagousia, Roditis, Zoumiatiko (Dimiat)
- **Red:** Bogialamades, Karnachalades, Keratsouda, Limnio, Mavroudi, Moschomavro, Pamidi (Pamid), Sefka

International grapes: Cabernet Sauvignon, Chardonnay, Cinsault, Grenache, Malvasia, Merlot, Muscat, Sauvignon Blanc, Syrah, Viognier

Thrace currently includes no PDOs.

- **PGIs**
  - PGI Avdira (ΠΓΕ Άβδηρα)
    - Still white, rosé, and red
  - PGI Evros (ΠΓΕ Έβρος)
    - Still white, rosé, and red
  - PGI Ismaros (ΠΓΕ Ίσμαρος)
    - Still white, rosé, and red
  - PGI Thrace (ΠΓΕ Θράκη)
    - Still white, rosé, and red

Recommended Producers:

Anatolikos Vineyards, Ktima Kikones, Ktima Vourvoukeli, Sgouridis Wines

Part 3

Where to Drink & Shop in Athens

Athens has one of the hottest wine scenes right now, so the below list is by no means exhaustive.

Note that the most disappointing part about the Athens wine scene is that bars often do not open until 16:00 or even 17:00.

Where to Drink:

Akra
Great restaurant but also offers and amazing selection of take-away wine!
address: Aminta 12, Pangrati
phone: +30 21 0725 1116

By the Glass
address: Souri 3, Athina 105 57, Greece
phone: +30 21 0323 2560

Caravin Wine & Wanderlust
address: Akamantos 11
phone: +30 21 1400 3962

Cinque Wine & Deli Monastiraki
address: Voreou 10
phone: +30 21 1410 8865

Cinque Wine & Deli Psirri
address: Agatharchou 15
phone: +30 21 5501 7853

Cinque Wine & Deli Acropolis
address: Drakou 3-5
phone: +30 21 0922 8378

Drunky Goat
address: Navarchou Nikodimou 5
phone: +30 21 0331 9966

Epta Martyres
address: Menechmou 3B

Gamay
address: Zoodochou Pigis 42
phone: +30 21 0380 7311

Heteroclito
Opens at 12:30!
address: Petraki 30, Athina
phone: +30 21 0323 9406

Lost Roots Wine Bar
address: Iraklidon 30
phone: +30 21 0345 7644

Oinoscent
address: Voulis 45-47
phone: +30 21 0322 9374

Psyche Wine Restaurant
address: Kornarou 4
phone: +30 21 0322 1271

Tanini Agapi Mou
address: *91 Ippokratous &, Methonis str*
phone: +30 *21 1115 0145*

Vintage
address: Mitropoleos 66
phone: +30 21 3029 6570

Warehouse
address: Valtetsiou 21
phone: +30 21 5540 8002

Warehouse Assamblage
address: Plateía Mitropóleos 8
phone: +30 21 0325 3503

Warehouse Co2
opens early!
address: Iperidou 1
phone: +30 21 0324 7048

Wine Bar 33
address: Αμύντα 4, Pl. Proskopon
phone: +30 69 4431 3187

Wine O'Clock
address: Lempesi 10
phone: +30 21 0924 9398

Wine With Eleni
address: Misaraliotou 20
phone : +30 693 412 5839

Wine Point
address: Porinou 2
phone: +30 21 0922 7050

Map!

Where to Shop:

Alfa Sigma Wine & Liquor Stores
website: e-alfasigma.gr/
address: Filellinon 14, Syntagma Square
phone number: +30 21 0321 1131

Cava Anthidis
website: anthidis.gr
address: Patriarchou Ioakim 45, Athina 106 76, Greece
phone: +30 21 0725 1050

Cava Canava
website: cavacanava.gr
address: Efroniou 63
phone: +30 21 0725 0444

Cava Nektar
website: cavanektar.gr
address: Ermou 121
phone: +30 21 0322 2216

Finewine Athens
website: finewine.gr
address: Thespidos 12
phone: +30 69 7432 0586

Greece And Grapes
online only, offers both shipping and in office pick up
website: greeceandgrapes.com

My Cava
website: mycava.gr
address: Efroniou 5, Pangrati
phone: +30 21 0724 4874

Οκκά Οινοπωλείο - Okka Wine Shop
website: okka.gr
address: Agiou Fanouriou 41
phone: +30 21 1405 4656

Wine Tunnel
address: Mitropoleos 32
phone: +30 21 0321 2346

Map!

Greek Wine Vocabulary

While even the smallest restaurant in Athens will have an English language food menu, it's surprising how many places don't yet have English language wine menus! Luckily, the majority of Athenians speak excellent English and can help you navigate menus and find something you'll like.

But, just in case, this short vocabulary list, combined with the grapes' Greek names included on the infographics, should help you navigate wine list and label basics.

If you want to attempt actually speaking Greek to order, don't be afraid of the language! Greek is pretty phonetic, so take your time to sound out the longer words and you'll be fine.

The Basics

wine - κρασί
white - λευκό
rose - ροζέ
red - κόκκινο
orange - πορτοκαλί
sparkling wine - αφρώδη κρασι
natural wine - φυσικά / αφύσικα κρασι
glass - ποτήρι
bottle - μπουκάλι

Winemaking

dry - ξηρό
sweet - γλυκό
oak - δρύινα
wooden barrels - ξύλινα βαρέλια
amphora - αμφορέα
clay amphora/pots - πήλινα δοχεία
skin contact - σε επαφή με τα στέμφυλα

Further Reading

Books:
- The Wines of Greece by Konstantinos Lazarakis MW
- The Wines of Santorini by Yiannis Karakasis MW
- The Vineyards & Wines of Greece 2017 by Yiannis Karakasis MW

Websites:
- Wines of Greece
- Yiannis Karakasis MW
- Wines of Crete
- Greek Wine World
- Greek Wine Roads
- The Greek Wine Experience
- Winemakers of Northern Greece
- Peloponnese Wine Roads
- Greece Is
- Greek Wine
- Wine-Searcher
- Wine Folly

Further Reading!

www.ingramcontent.com/pod-product-compliance
Lightning Source LLC
Chambersburg PA
CBHW061755120626
46550CB00005B/2002